Atheist comments on the

"I found the God Delusion quite a depressing read because a) the arguments did seem banal and not in any way inspiring b) many of the criticisms of religion I could only help agreeing with.... I couldn't quite believe that someone so clever would use such biased and naïve arguments. I thought I was missing something. You've helped me see through it...."

"Robertson is a prat. And not only a PRAT, but a dangerous PRAT. A complete loser. I've never read such a dogmatic, vicious diatribe as this. WHEN WILL THEISTS LIKE ROBERTSON actually provide some EMPIRICAL EVIDENCE of their own – something we can really scrutinize and say – 'Hey! You know, there could be a God, judged on this evidence'."

"Bravo David Robertson, Not only did you take the time to read The God Delusion You also took the time to write a long article about your reaction, and now you join this discussion."

"Wow, this is an intelligent and well-crafted view of RD's book. I can see that it really got to most readers of this site as well, seeing as it was posted 2 days ago and already has a comment pagination level of 5, and most of the comments are just stating that the writer of this entry is wrong and a dumb stupid-head. I love it when things get stirred up. Please keep it up!"

"I'm impressed that some of the people here bother to debate this Robertson nincompoop. He is clearly out of his mind and beyond reason and logic. If you do debate him, stop respecting his delusions, however eloquent he puts them, and please approach *him with the scorn and contempt that he deserves. Dawkins refuses to debate this sort of weirdness because it gives the person with the sick mind the impression that there really is something to debate."*

"I'd like to say thank you for your articulate responses to all of these (sometimes hostile) questions. I am definitely an atheist but I really appreciate some good, healthy, well written debate."

THE DAWKINS LETTERS
CHALLENGING ATHEIST MYTHS DAVID ROBERTSON

CHRISTIAN
FOCUS

ISBN 1-84550-261-2
ISBN 978-1-84550-261-4

Copyright © David Robertson 2007

10 9 8 7 6 5 4 3 2 1

Published in 2007
by
Christian Focus Publications, Ltd.,
Geanies House, Fearn, Ross-shire,
IV20 1TW, Great Britain.

www.christianfocus.com

Cover design by Moose77.com

Printed and bound by
Nørhaven Paperback A/S, Denmark

THE DAWKINS LETTERS
CHALLENGING ATHEIST MYTHS **DAVID ROBERTSON**

Contents

INTRODUCTORY LETTER TO THE READER

Dear Reader,

The book you are reading is a collection of open review letters written in response to Professor Richard Dawkins in the winter of 2006/7 concerning his book *The God Delusion*.[1] Richard Dawkins is a brilliant and well-known British scientist. He is the Charles Simonyi Professor of the Public Understanding of Science at the University of Oxford and one of the best popularisers of science. However, in recent years he has become better known as Britain's most famous atheist. His most recent works have taken an increasingly strident and militant anti-religious position, his previous book being *A Devil's Chaplain*, which is a collection of essays many of which attack religious beliefs,[2] being followed by this, his most important work.

The God Delusion has hit the American and British markets at a time when religion is never far from the front pages. For those who grew up in the 1960s thinking that they were witnessing the death throes of religion it has been something of a revelation and concern that the 'march of progress' seems to have been impeded by a resurgence of 'irrational' religion and superstition. There is considerable worry that 9/11 and the rise of Islamic fundamentalism is being matched by a rise in Christian fundamentalism. In Europe this is seen by many

[1] Bantam Press (2006)
[2] Weidenfeld and Nicholson (2003)

as being a significant motivating factor in the 'War on Terror'. In the US there appears to be the beginnings of a backlash against the perceived power of the Christian Right. It is into this climate of hostility, religious confusion and fear that Dawkins' clarion call to atheists to 'come out' and organise is addressed. It is a message that is being welcomed by many and is causing considerable interest. *The God Delusion* has been on the New York Times bestseller list for several months and is well on its way to becoming a million seller in Britain. This despite a significant number of hostile and negative reviews (by no means all of them from religious protagonists). It is a powerful, well-written book which despite its many weaknesses is having a considerable influence.

It is also generating a response. Alister McGrath and his wife, Joanna, have published *The Dawkins Delusion?*[3] in response. Many articles, newspaper columns and reviews have already been written. So why add to them with this small book? There have been a number of academic responses to the various accusations made by Dawkins and I am sure that there will be more. However, for many the damage will have been done and those who do not read academic books will still be left with the impressions and the myths. On the other hand there will be those who from a religious perspective, have a kind of knee jerk reaction and respond to Dawkins' vehemence in kind. Whilst this may appeal to those in their own constituencies, it is unlikely to do anything other than reinforce the impression that religious people are deluded. And of course there will be many who think this should just be left alone and ignored. After all, is anything ever settled by argument? I suspect that you are not in the latter grouping, otherwise you would not be reading this book.

Given that there have been and will be many responses, why add to them with this collection of letters? I guess the answer

[3] *The Dawkins Delusion?* SPCK (2007)

is simply that many people will not have the time, inclination or money to read about every single subject that Dawkins addresses. My aim is to present one person's response to Dawkins and to do so from a wide and personal perspective. My aim is not to convert, nor to insult, nor even to defend. Rather it is to challenge some of the basic myths that Dawkins uses and encourages in his book, in order that you may think and consider these things for yourself. If you are interested in reading about or even discussing these immensely important subjects further, then at the end you will find a reading list and some suggestions.

A word about the style of these letters. Some will consider that they are too angry, others that they are not angry enough; some wonder whether humour is appropriate, others will ask, 'what humour?!' It will be helpful to remember that these are personal letters, not an academic discourse, nor an exercise in English grammar.

I am deeply grateful to those who have read and commented on the letters (the wounds of a friend are faithful!). In particular I would like to thank Dr Elias Medeiros, Bill Schweitzer, Dr Grant Macaskill, Dr Iain D. Campbell, Gary Aston, Dr Deuan Jones, David Campbell, Dr Sam Logan, Will Traub, Dr Cees Dekker, Nigel Anderson, Dr Phil Ryken, Iver Martin, Alex Macdonald, Alastair Donald and Dr Ligon Duncan. Whether scientists, philosophers or theologians, British, American or European you have all provoked, encouraged and stimulated. I am especially grateful to my editor, Dr Bob Carling, whose patience and suggestions have been invaluable. The final responsibility for what is written, including any errors or misjudgements, is, of course, mine.

I am not a scientist, and I am not a well-known Oxford scholar with an international reputation. There are many people who will be able to go into detail and answer Dawkins' many accusations in greater depth than this book even attempts. Some of my own personal background comes across in the letters but perhaps at this stage it will be helpful for you to know that I am a 44-year-old minister in a Presbyterian Church in Scotland. Having been brought up on a farm in the Highlands of Scotland, I studied history at the University of Edinburgh and then theology at the Free Church College. I have been a minister for 20 years, 14 of them in the city of Dundee. I am a Christian minister with a deep interest in what Dawkins calls the cultural *zeitgeist* – the way our culture is going. I am a frequent visitor to the USA and Europe with a particular interest in bringing the Good News, the Gospel, to our post-Christian society. I believe that the Gospel is something that is relevant and vital for all people in all cultures at all times and it has been my privilege to see people from many different backgrounds come to know, love and have their lives changed by Jesus Christ.

As a deeply committed Christian I am disturbed by the attacks that Dawkins makes on God and the Bible, and astonished that his attacks are taken so seriously. I believe that he is appealing not to people's intelligence and knowledge but rather to their ignorance. This series of letters is presented to the reader in order to challenge some of the atheist myths that Dawkins taps into and feeds. Each letter deals with a chapter of the book and each highlights at least one atheist myth. I call them atheist myths because they are beliefs that are widely held or assumed without necessarily having been thought through or evidenced.

If you are a Christian then I presume you are reading this because you want to think about some of the issues involved and like me want to reflect on how your faith fits into modern society. If you are not yet a Christian (or you are unsure, or a follower of another faith) I hope that you will benefit from reading these letters. My prayer is that you will be stimulated, challenged, provoked and most of all drawn to consider the claims of Jesus Christ.

Finally, I would like to thank my congregation St Peter's Free Church, for their love, support and understanding over the years. Likewise I thank my wife and best friend, Annabel, and our children, Andrew, Becky and Emma Jane who are constant reminders to me of the grace and goodness of God.

This book is dedicated to the glory of God and in memory of the many millions who lost their lives in the wars and injustices of the Failed Atheist 20th Century.

David A. Robertson
Dundee 2007

LETTER 1 –
THE MYTH OF THE HIGHER
CONSCIOUSNESS

Dear Dr Dawkins,

I hope you will forgive me writing to you but I have just finished reading your book and it was very frustrating. There was so much in it that I could identify with and yet so much that was to my mind just simply wrong. I would love to discuss it with you, or with those who are your disciples, but I'm afraid that I am not an Oxford Don, I don't have the access to the media you do, and I am not part of the Establishment. And of course you have stated that you do not discuss with 'fundamentalists' or those who believe in revelation or supernaturalism. Given that the subject about which you are so vehement is the whole question of supernaturalism and whether there is a God or not, do you not think it is kind of loading the dice to discuss this only with those who already share your presuppositions?

And then there is the problem of what you call 'the Higher Consciousness'. You argue that those who share your views have been raised to a greater level of consciousness. Your book is written to make atheists 'loud and proud' that they have had their consciousness raised, whilst also seeking to raise the consciousness of those of us who have been left behind. This reminds me of the story of the Emperor's New Clothes. The Emperor is told by a couple of 'tailors' that they have produced a set of new clothes for him which can only be seen by the enlightened and wise (those who have had their consciousness raised). Of course not wanting to appear stupid he and all his courtiers state that they can see the wonderful and stunning new clothes. It is only when the emperor is wandering naked through the streets and a small boy cries out, 'The Emperor has no clothes', that the people realise the truth. I think your notion that atheists are those who have had their consciousness raised, and that they are *de facto* more intelligent, rational and honest than other human beings, is a myth on a par with the Emperor's New Clothes.

Of course I realise that many people who buy your book will already be converts – they already share your faith and will be looking for reassurance or confirmation. You are preaching to the choir. This is rather obvious even from the people who write the blurb on the jacket cover, admittedly not normally unbiased objective judges. Stephen Pinker, Brian Eno, Derren Brown and Philip Pullman all wax lyrical about your book – but then this is hardly surprising given that they are convinced atheists already. Pullman wants your anti-faith book to be put into every faith school (which is a little surprising, given that you make such a fuss about children being indoctrinated – unless of course atheist indoctrination is OK). Eno says it is 'a book for the new millennium, one in which we may be released from lives dominated by the supernatural'. Heady stuff. But best of all is Derren Brown who affirms *The God Delusion* as his 'favourite book of all time'. It is 'a heroic and life-changing work'. He hopes that those who are 'secure and intelligent enough to see the value of questioning their beliefs will be big enough and strong enough to read this book'.

Well, I have read it. I did expect to be challenged. You are after all one of the world's top three intellectuals' (as the book jacket reminds us). Of course *The God Delusion* was well written, very entertaining and passionate. But at an intellectual and logical level it really misses the mark. Most of the arguments are of sixth-form schoolboy variety and shot through with a passionate anti-religious vehemence. What is disturbing is that your fundamentalist atheism will actually be taken seriously by some and will be used to reinforce their already prejudged anti-religion and anti-Christian stance. Your 'arguments' will be repeated *ad nauseam* in newspaper letters, columns, opinion pages, pubs and dinner tables throughout the land. You will forgive me saying this but it seems remarkably similar to the kind of thing that 'intellectuals' were putting out in 1930s Germany about the Jews and Judaism. Just as they claimed the Jews were responsible for all the ills in Weimar Germany, so according to your book religious people are responsible for the majority of ills in today's society.

Along with John Lennon you want us to 'imagine' a world with no religion and no God. A world that you claim would have no suicide bombers (despite the fact that the most suicide attacks have been by the secular Sri Lankan Tamil Tigers), no crusades, no 9/11, no Israeli/Palestinian wars, etc. By the way, John Lennon was one of my heroes and I loved *Imagine*. Then I grew up and realised that it took a great deal of imagination to take seriously a song which spoke of imagining a world 'with no possessions too', written by a man who lived in a mansion and had an abundance of possessions, whilst there were millions dying from lack of resources. It seems to me that your vision/imagination is almost as unrealistic as Lennon's.

I want to write a letter in response to each of your chapters. As you correctly point out each of them deals with issues that are fundamental to our existence, meaning and well-being as humans. But let me finish off this first letter by looking at a couple of other things you state in your own introduction.

You claim that your book is for those who have been brought up in a particular religious faith and now either no longer believe it, or are unhappy in it and want out. You want to raise the consciousness of such people to the extent that they can realise that they can get out. Do most people not already know that it is perfectly possible to leave a religion and not suffer any significant consequences? Of course if you are in an Islamic society that is not true (but your book is not really directed at Islam) and I realise that for some in the US admitting you are an atheist is political suicide, but overall most people are free to change their beliefs. I was brought up in a religious home and knew from a very young age that not only was it possible to leave, but that for many people it would be considered normal. I fought my own battles so that I could be free to think for myself. But it was not only, nor even primarily, against the religious teachings of my parents or others (and I did fight against them), but also the patronising expectations of teachers, media and others who just assumed that the only reason anyone would be religious was because of parental influence, brainwashing and a weak mind. You know the real relief came when I realised I could be a Christian *and* think for myself *and* seek to make a difference in the world; and that I did not have to buy into all the quirks and cultural nuances of religious groups, nor the fundamentalism of the secularists who just knew that they were right.

I cannot think of a single career option in Britain where being an atheist would place you at a disadvantage (unless you are thinking of becoming a member of the clergy – although current form suggests that even there you could get away with it!). However, there are many people for whom admitting they are 'religious' is a severe block to their career and life. Those who seek to be Christian politicians, singers, businessmen, teachers and social workers often face significant prejudice and irrational fear. It is sometimes advantageous to deny one's faith or even to leave it. Being a Christian is more often than not a stumbling block to one's chosen career path, rather than being an atheist.

Of course there are those who belong to cults that exercise a form of mind control tantamount to brainwashing, but surely even you would not argue that every religious person is in that category? You seem to think that anyone who is religious is actually at a lower level of consciousness and needs to be set free by becoming an atheist. Of course you offer no empirical evidence for this. Like much of the book, it is a presupposition (even a prejudice) that does not appear to be founded on anything other than you would like it to be so. Have you ever thought that there might be many others who are in the opposite position – brought up in an atheistic secular society and discovering that they can actually believe in God? Would you give them the freedom to do so? What would you do if your daughter turned out to be a Bible believing Christian? Would you disown her? Would you even allow her that choice? Or have you done your best to inoculate her against the virus of religion? I remember one young man, highly intelligent, who came to a Christianity Explored group. When he was asked his religious position he said, 'I'm an atheist, but I'm beginning to have my doubts'. I laughed. A backslidden atheist! I thought that was quite neat. Maybe there are a lot more of them than you think. You ought to be careful about the raising of consciousness – maybe people will become tired of your modernist certainties and instead find refuge in the clear fresh air of Jesus Christ!

I also smiled when I read your complaint that atheists were persecuted and misunderstood. You contrast the current situation of atheists with the situation of homosexuals a couple of decades ago and suggest that just as 'gays' had to 'come out' so also 'brights' (the rather hopeful and somewhat arrogant newly coined name for atheists) need to come out of the closet and establish their place in society. I had not noticed that atheists were particularly silent or poorly represented in British society (or even American). In Britain all our government institutions, media outlets and educational establishments are primarily secularist. The National Secular Society get a far bigger exposure than the vast majority of Christian churches – despite the fact that most secular societies could fit their members into a phone box. Even when the Prime Minister was asked a relatively innocuous question about whether he prays, his media minder Alasdair Campbell felt compelled to point out, 'we don't do God'. Atheism and secularism are, without doubt, the prevailing philosophies of those who consider themselves 'the elite'.

You were given the immense privilege of having editorial control of your own TV series *The Root of all Evil*. Can you tell me when an Evangelical Christian was last given the opportunity by a national TV channel to produce a film demonstrating the evils of atheism? Do you not think that in an open and democratic society when you are allowed to make a 'documentary' attacking whole groups of people they should at least be allowed some right of reply? Of course, that is not going to happen, because, as you well know, those who are primarily in charge of our media outlets are those who share many of your presuppositions and prefer to make programmes which present Christians as either weak ineffective Anglican vicars, or tub-thumping American Right Wing Evangelists who want to hang gays. It is propaganda – not truth, not reason, not debate and most certainly not fair.

At a meeting of BBC Executives in 2006 it was reported[4] that the policy of the Corporation is that secularism is the *only* philosophy to which others must eventually come. Other philosophies and belief systems can be tolerated but they must never be allowed any real say in the BBC. Apparently some had the audacity to suggest that perhaps the BBC should recognise

[4] *Daily Mail* (24 October 2006); *Prospect* Magazine (November 2006)

that secularism is *a* philosophy and not *the* philosophy. I hope that you will support such pluralistic open-mindedness.

The atheist revival is now being challenged from all sides. Having had a century of elitist domination and control many in the Western World are beginning to wake up to the fact that the secular emperor has no clothes. The 20th century can truly be called the Failed Atheist Century. Can I recommend that you read an excellent book on this subject, written by one of your Oxford colleagues, Niall Ferguson, *The War of the World: History's Age of Hatred*?[5] He shares your evolutionary secularist presuppositions, but his account of the 20th century is a stunning indictment of the failure of secularism and 'science' to bring peace on earth.

Your book comes across as a desperate attempt to shore up atheism's crumbling defences. Ironically it reminds me of some in the Church who, faced with what seems to be overwhelming odds and staring defeat in the face, issue evangelistic tracts, articles and books which are designed to shore up the faith of the faithful rather than being aimed at the conversion of unbelievers. *The God Delusion* fits nicely into that category. I am sure you will delight your disciples, establishing what they already believe, but I very much doubt you will make any impact on others who are less fixed in their opinions and who really are seekers after truth. What I do appreciate is that, unlike the irrational and the lazy who want to deny its existence, you admit that there is such a thing as truth. You may laugh at the idea that the truth is ultimately found in Jesus Christ. But I remain an optimist. I believe not only in truth but also in the power of God and his Holy Spirit to bring enlightenment to even the darkest mind. So there is still hope for us both.

Yours, etc.

David

[5] Allen Lane (2006)

LETTER 2 –
THE MYTH OF GODLESS BEAUTY

Dear Dr Dawkins,

Thanks for posting my letter on your website. That was very unexpected – almost as unexpected as the response from some of your fellow atheists, as evidenced on your message board. Although some were intelligent, thoughtful and expressed their disagreement in a constructive and stimulating way, a surprising number reacted with all the vehemence of religious believers whose sacred holy book was being blasphemed. I thought I had seen vitriol before, but this lot would take some beating. Anyway it's not fair to judge a belief system by those of its advocates who are eccentric, extreme and in need of some kind of therapy. Please remember that when you discuss Christianity.

I have also found it very interesting watching your 'tour of the USA'.[6] It struck me that there are a number of similarities between your tour and some revivalist TV evangelist rallies. You have mass rallies to the converted (which you totally control). You mock those who disagree with you and refuse to engage with them in any constructive way. You demonise those who do not share your point of view. You (or your advocates) exult at your book being in the New York Times Bestseller list and encourage people to go out and buy copies for friends and even, in the latest campaign, copies for politicians. Fans are also

[6] See www.richarddawkins.net

19

encouraged to watch the latest YouTube of 'Dawkins Destroying Dumb Fundies'. I can even obtain special edition jacket covers and website banners. It's highly entertaining – in the same way that 'Reality' or even 'God TV' can be, but it hardly constitutes rational argument and discussion.

Anyway, let us leave aside this rather commercial and politicised behaviour and not indulge in the view that because the methods are suspect, the message must be false. Let's go to chapter one of your book. It's a great beginning, well written, well argued, informative and, much to my surprise, very persuasive. This is probably my favourite chapter. There is so much I can identify with and even say 'Amen' to! However, whilst I can accept and am convinced by some of the premises you state, I am less than convinced by some of the conclusions that you draw.

A Sense of Wonder

This is a key concept and you deal with it brilliantly. Many of us have been there. I remember as a boy being transfixed by the stars as I walked home across the Morrich Moor in the Scottish Highlands. I lived on top of Nigg cliffs where I often sat looking out over the Cromarty Firth (an inlet leading to the North Sea), being utterly amazed at the beauty and variety in nature: the seagulls, the blue sea, the purple heather, the yellow gorse, the seals and even the occasional dolphin. It felt like paradise (even with the old World War 2 gun emplacements still deeply embedded in the cliffs). If you don't feel a sense of wonder in such an environment you ain't got no soul. You have obviously had the same experience – as I suspect most human beings have. But you interpret it differently.

You think that to believe that God has created and is responsible for such magnificence is somehow to demean the beauty and explain away the sense of wonder. I must admit, that thought was not something new to me. I tried really hard to think the same thing. It seemed to me also that the 'gods' of religion were somehow trivial compared to such beauty and grace. And here's the rub. They are. But neither could I replace them with humans. Darwin's quotation, which you cite, is an example of human arrogance at its worst:

Thus, from the war of nature, from famine and death, the most exalted object which we are capable of conceiving, namely the production of the higher animals, directly follows.

Is that really it? Is mankind the most exalted object that we are capable of conceiving? I remember a good man saying that if Jesus Christ was not real he would worship the man who invented him! Was I to be faced with the choice of man-made idols or human beings as the apex of creation? Neither was satisfactory. But where did this beauty come from? Why did I feel it? No one gives a better answer than Solomon, the wisest man who ever lived: 'God has made everything beautiful in its time. He has also set eternity in the hearts of men; yet they cannot fathom what God has done from beginning to end' (Ecclesiastes 3:11).

I tried really hard to be an atheist, or at least an agnostic, but I just couldn't get there. One New Year's Eve I even prayed to a God I was not sure even existed: 'Oh God, if you are there, show me and I will serve you the rest of my life.' There was no voice from heaven. No flashing light. And as far as I could see the prayer remained unanswered – until one Sunday I decided that after all I would go to Church. I went to a small Scottish Presbyterian church beside the sea, down from those same cliffs. As I listened to the sound of the plain singing of the psalms of the Bible and heard the waves of the sea splashing against the walls of the Church, it struck me what a fool I had been. Of course God existed. Nothing else made sense. You cannot explain beauty or evil, creation or humanity, time or space, without God. Or at least you can, but to my mind the materialistic, atheistic explanation is emotionally, spiritually and above all intellectually inadequate. Indeed, it takes a great deal of faith to be an atheist.

By the way, I should point out that there is an interesting connection here between religion and science. Across the cliffs, on the other side of the Firth, is a small village called Cromarty. About 150 years ago there lived an extraordinary man called Hugh Miller. He was a genius. He had your gift for writing and he was also one of the founding fathers of modern geology. His book *The Old Red Sandstone* and *In the Footprints of the Creator* are still classics. He was absolutely convinced that the geological evidence was for an old earth. Miller was an elder in the Free Church, editor of its newspaper and a strong political advocate for the Highlands peasants who were being cleared from their homes (in yet another example of the Selfish Gene principle at work). He loved science and found in it, not a contradiction of the Bible, but a complementarity.

You cite Carl Sagan from his *Pale Blue Dot*.[7] It is worth quoting in full again.

How is it that hardly any major religion has looked at science and concluded, 'This is better than we thought! The Universe is much bigger than our prophets said, grander, more subtle, more elegant?' Instead they say, 'No, no, no! My god is a little god, and I want him to stay that way.' A religion, old or new, that stressed the magnificence of the Universe as revealed by modern science might be able to draw forth reserves of reverence and awe hardly tapped by the conventional faiths.

[7] Ballantine Books (1997)

That is brilliant. I would shout Hallelujah if it were not for the fact that this would immediately caricature me as a tub-thumping evangelical! The modern Christian church in the West has, on the whole, to hold up its hands and admit guilt. *Mea culpa.* We have too often reduced God to a formula, belief to a system and worship to a happy-clappy, feel-good floor show. Our God *is* too small. But that is because he is *our* God and not the God of the Bible.

Not long after becoming a Christian I came to understand and appreciate the writings of John Calvin and others who followed his particular line of biblical teaching. I loved it. They portrayed the God of the Bible as magnificent, powerful, deep, glorious, sovereign, worthy of praise and the creator of this amazing, vast and complex universe. They did not put him in a box, indeed they argued that by very definition God could not be boxed. Which is what led men like the 19th-century Scottish theologian Thomas Chalmers to enquire and think 'outside the box'. Chalmers even wrote a best-selling book entitled *Astronomical Discourses* which discussed the possibility of life on other planets.

When I first became a Christian I thought I had it all worked out. I had God in a box. I had Jesus. But as I grew and matured I realised that instead of me being in charge of the paddling pool, all I had done was dip my big toe into the ocean of God's knowledge, love and being. The boxed small God does result in an antagonistic view to anything (including science) that will not fit into that box. But the unboxed God, the God of the Bible, allows us – no, encourages us – to explore his creation, to climb the heights and scale the depths. I think of the award-winning, brilliant biochemist who heard me waxing lyrical about the wonder of God in the stars and spoke to me afterwards. He told me that in his work, studying some of the smallest observable things known to man, he too was seeing the wonder and glory of God.

Some of your followers have been trying to contrast science and Christianity with the rather foolish challenge, 'science has given us cars/toasters/spacecraft, etc. What has religion ever given us?' It is foolish because they are making a false dichotomy between science and Christianity as though science is one belief system and Christianity another. No. The difference is not in terms of science but in terms of philosophy and belief. The danger of the position that you are advocating is that you want to drive a wedge between science and religion to suit your own philosophy (of course in that you are joined by some religious fundamentalists). But your position is philosophical, not scientific. To put it more plainly, the reason that you are an atheist is not because you are driven there by scientific fact, but because that is your philosophy. You use science to justify it but then many religious people also use science to justify their position. The question is not science but rather the presuppositions that we bring to science.

Let me leave this section on wonder by suggesting that you could do a lot worse than read one of the greatest philosophical minds that America has ever produced – Jonathan Edwards. If any human being grasped something of the grandeur of God, it was Edwards. Take this from his work *The Nature of True Virtue*:

> For as God is infinitely the Greatest Being, so he is … infinitely the most beautiful and excellent. All the beauty to be found throughout the whole creation is but a reflection of the diffused beams of that Being who hath an infinite fullness of brightness and glory. God is the foundation of all beauty and glory.[8]

8 1765. Republished by Banner of Truth (1974)

A Sense of Religion

Now let's turn to your use of the term 'religious'. I agree with most of what you say here. It is all about how we use and understand the term 'God'. I accept fully that too many Christians have been guilty of selective quotation, and circulation of urban myths, in order to prove that this or that famous person was either a Christian or had a deathbed conversion. Your evidence concerning Einstein seems absolutely convincing and it means that I will have to be careful about using such quotes as 'Science without religion is lame, religion without science is blind.' Although I am convinced that you are right about this and indeed about many 'religious' people who only use the term 'god' as a synonym for their own 'religious' feelings or sense of wonder, yet I am not convinced that this sense of wonder is something that is just a product of our natural being/environment.

You state that naturalists believe that everything is physical. I think of one highly intelligent chemist who when challenged on this admitted that love, hate, beauty, spirituality and so on were all in the end 'just' chemical reactions. This seems to me a profoundly depressing minimalist view of the universe and of human life. Of course, if you could prove it and evidence that there was no personal God then I guess we would have to live with it. But you cannot. Your view, that the universe is only physical, is a hypothesis and one that is largely based on wishful thinking. In fact, your position is a kind of 'science of the gaps': there are certain things you observe, you cannot really explain them scientifically and you do not want to resort to explaining them spiritually (because you have a basic philosophical presupposition that nothing exists except matter), so rather than leave any gaps (through which you fear a small god might slip) you basically expand your scientific knowledge so that it becomes a theory of everything – and you conveniently shut out anything that does not fit in that box. Ironically, the very thing that you accuse Christians of doing with God, putting him into a box, is something that you are in danger of doing with science, creating a human construct based upon your anti-religious presuppositions which, whilst designed to shut out God, actually ends up boxing in science.

Whilst I agree in general with the section on the use of the term 'god' there are a couple of remarks that do not hold up. For example you state that, 'the notion that religion is a proper field, in which one might claim expertise, is one that should not go unquestioned'. Here your hatred for religion has gone slightly over the top. Given that the majority of the world over the majority of history has been, and still is, religious, one would have thought that it is a reasonable field for study and that there are some who can claim some degree of expertise in it. Indeed, your dismissal of any who do is a neat trick that will allow you to critique religions and religious books without having to resort to any kind of academic scholarship because after all religion is not a proper field. This, then, allows you to get away with simplistic statements such as 'pantheism is just sexed up atheism'. Given your earlier definition of atheists as being naturalists who hold to the notion that there is only the material you will find that there are many pantheists who are not atheists. They believe in numerous spirits, gods and non-material things.

I also find that you have an interesting use of quotations. You cite letters from an American Roman Catholic and the president of a historical society. I am sure they are not the only letters sent by those who disagreed with Einstein's views but they are the ones you selected. Why? Because they allow you to imply or assert that Christians are either ignorant or full of 'intellectual and moral cowardice'. It is the classic *ad hominem* argument: look how stupid these Christians are, therefore God cannot exist. I, as a Christian, do not agree with either the tone or the substance of those letters, and I know of very few Christian scholars who would (but you already covered your bases with that one by declaring there is no such thing as Christian scholarship!). In particular, the oft-cited, but biblically false assertion, 'as everyone knows, religion is based on Faith, not knowledge'. I would argue the opposite – faith without knowledge is blind and stupid. Biblical faith is in a person. If you do not know about that person you cannot have faith in him.

How would you feel if I took some of the more ludicrous and ignorant comments from some of the atheists on your website and used them as an example of how atheism rots the brain? It would not be fair or honest.

One final thought. You claim to be a religious non-believer. That to me is the worst of both worlds. I hate religion. I think that Marx was in some sense right – religion has far too often been used as the opiate of the people. In the name of religion a great deal of evil and harm has been done. Ironically I believe that religion *per se* has brought us a great deal of harm. But I do believe. I believe in the God of the Bible. I find that his revelation of himself in both the creation and Scripture is wonderfully liberating and best fits the facts as far as I can see them. You may aspire to be a religious non-believer. I am delighted to be a non-religious believer.

All the best,
David

Dear Dr Dawkins,

I would like to apologise if I am in any way misrepresenting your position. It is not intentional. I disagree with what you say and it would therefore be pretty pointless to write about what you are not saying. However, I am becoming more and more convinced that your position is primarily a philosophical and religious position, rather than one you are driven to by science. That also appears to be the position of many of your fellow atheists on your website, whose reaction to the criticism has been akin to some religious fundamentalists I know.

You have a central thesis, that science proves, in so far as it is possible, that God does not exist and that belief in him is a delusion. But you surround that thesis with a whole army of smaller arguments, such as the nature of religion, supposed errors in the Bible, hypocrisy in the Church, etc. These have the effect of, apparently, reinforcing your main argument whilst at the same time allowing your supporters to complain, when these surrounding arguments are challenged, that the challenger's views are irrational and stupid because they do not address the central thesis.

Some Christians want to argue in the same vein – of course God exists and anyone who denies otherwise is ignorant, irrational, etc. Thus we end up with the dialogue of the blind and the deaf. Which is pretty dumb. What I am trying to do in these letters is deal with all the secondary arguments in the order that you bring them up in the book. As we deconstruct these, we can see that many of them are either red herrings, irrelevant or just simply wrong. We are then left with the central kernel of your argument, which, shod of this scaffolding, is seen to be naked and without any significant support. The atheist emperor is seen to have no clothes.

A number of years ago when I was a student at the University of Edinburgh I was involved in a debate with members of the Feminist Society. It left a profound impression. Amongst the other 'rational' arguments used to prove that men were no longer needed was the classic 'the nuclear bomb is the ultimate phallic symbol and therefore all men are less than nice people' (I paraphrase slightly for the sake of decency!). At one point they even threw flour and eggs at me and my colleague, yelling that we were MCPs (Male Chauvinist Pigs) just because we stated that there was a role for men on the earth. It would all have been good fun if it were not for the fact that some of them really believed the hyperbole and nonsense they were spouting. I wonder whether they had had a bad experience of some man or other and this was then being projected on to all men and into some kind of radical feminist philosophy.

I had a sense of *deja vu* whilst looking on your website. I'm afraid that many atheists seem to work from the same premise – their own experience, as indeed many Christians, including myself, also do. However, I am sure you would recognise that whilst experience is an important factor it cannot be the determining factor in ascertaining what is objective truth. Many have had a bad experience of religion in some form or other; therefore they project that on to every religion or religious person. And when someone like you comes along and provides what seems to be a cast-iron intellectual justification they seize it like an alcoholic seizes the bottle. Not only are their feelings justified but also they are suddenly part of the 'higher intelligence' or 'greater consciousness'. The trouble is the argument you use and how you approach your subject.

I have received several complaints from some of your followers that I have not addressed the central question in my two previous letters, namely the existence of God. 'Go, on,' they say. 'Prove it.' They then complain that I have talked about the issues you talk about. What they do is a simple and false equation. They state there is only the material and that the only thing that can be called proof is a material proof. In effect, they are asking me to prove God as a chemical equation. 'If you can't do this,' they say, 'there is no God.' This is the ultimate in circular argument. But it fails at two levels. First of all its presupposition and assertion/assumption, that everything is chemical or the result of chemical reaction, is itself an unprovable assertion. Second, it is not an assertion that fits with the observable facts around us. Indeed, it requires a great deal of special pleading before one can honestly come to the position that religion is just a chemical reaction, beauty is just a chemical reaction, evil likewise and the sense of God also. Furthermore, the logical consequences of such a belief are disastrous. We end up with the absurdity of man as God – the most highly evolved chemical reaction.

As I have already indicated, most of your book does not seek to prove its central 'everything is chemical' hypothesis, quite simply because it is not provable. So in order to protect and prop up the faith of your fellow atheists and encourage them to 'come out' you do two things. First, you defend atheism from the charge that it leads to various negative consequences. And second, you go on the attack – ridiculing, mocking and denigrating the beliefs of those who do not share your presuppositions. You realise that this opens you to the charge of being aggressive, arrogant and even harmful to your own cause. Thus, you seek to defend your methodology to other atheists. Indeed, there is a fascinating subtext in your book – the in-house debate within atheist circles. In the Church of the Blessed Atheist it seems as though there is a doctrinal dispute that could result in a split. On the one hand there is the Respect party (the 'niceies'); on the other the Ridicule party (the 'nasties'). Both factions believe that religion is evil and that anyone who believes in God is a superstitious anti-rationalist. The Respects argue that you have to be nice to people to win them. The Ridicules regard this as cowardice, having more to do with keeping the peace, rather than standing up for the truth.

If I belonged to your religion I would be inclined towards your side. And so would the apostle Paul who argued that if the resurrection was not true then Christians should 'be pitied more than all men' (1 Corinthians 15:19). As would the prophet Elijah who mocked and ridiculed the prophets of Baal as they prayed, danced and cut themselves in order to arouse their God – 'At noon Elijah began to taunt them. "Shout louder!" he said. "Surely he is a god! Perhaps he is deep in thought, or busy, or travelling. Maybe he is sleeping and must be awakened!' (1 Kings 18:27). Even Jesus was fairly scathing towards those who peddled religious untruths and myths.

It is in this context that the last part of your first chapter argues over the question of respect. Your main point is that you think it unfair and illogical that just because something is deemed to be religious it should be treated with kid gloves. You cite with glowing approval your friend the late Douglas Adams: 'Religion … has certain ideas at the heart of it which we call sacred or holy or whatever. What it means is: "Here is an idea or notion that you're not allowed to say anything bad about; you're just not. Why not? – because you're not."' I agree with the main substance of your argument – just because someone cites their view as religious does not *de facto* entitle it to respect. Where both you and Adams miss the point is that you fail to acknowledge that every society, whether overtly religious or not, has its shibboleths. There are some things that one is not allowed to question at least not without losing one's job, position, etc. And that is as true in a secular society (perhaps even more so) as it is in a religious one.

This is seen in another example you bring up, that of Christian groups on campuses suing their universities because the universities are harassing these groups for their perceived anti-homosexual stance. As it happens, I am writing this alongside a copy of *The Times* (18 November 2006) which on its front page reports on a similar situation in the UK. Edinburgh University for example has banned the Christian Union from teaching a course about sex and relationships because it promotes 'homophobia'. I have seen this course (entitled *Pure*) and it does no such thing (unless you are prepared to make the completely unwarranted and bigoted assumption that if one does not agree with something one automatically is phobic about it and hates the people who do agree with it). *Pure* encourages the biblical teaching that sex should be within the context of marriage and that marriage should be between one man and one woman. Likewise the Christian Union in Heriot Watt University has been banned because its core beliefs 'discriminate against non-Christians and those of other faiths'. The 150-strong CU in Birmingham was suspended for refusing to alter its constitution to allow non-Christians to preach at its meetings and to amend its literature to include references to gays, lesbians, bisexuals and those of 'transgender' sexuality (one wonders what the logic was for leaving out polygamists, bestialists or paedophiles?). The point is simply this – not whether you agree with their particular view of sexuality but whether they are to have the freedom to express that view. Some secularists in the US and the UK seem prepared to take this matter of sexuality and use it the way that Douglas Adams describes. You are not allowed to question it or to have a different viewpoint and when you ask why, you are just told – that is the way it is. I would hope that you would accept that Christian Unions have the right to determine what they believe themselves, as I would Atheist societies, and that nothing should be imposed on people because 'that is just the way things are.'

Going off on another bypath meadow that you set up, you assert that conflicts in areas such as Northern Ireland, Bosnia and Iraq should be seen as religious wars and not ethnic ones. Whilst I fully agree that religion is sometimes the cause of the most appalling behaviour in people, it is more often the case that religion is the excuse rather than the cause for ethnic divisions and wars. I have met people, for example, from both sides of the divide in Northern Ireland who were involved in 'the Troubles'. Not one of them thought that they were rioting or killing for 'God'. It was for their 'community', their 'tribe' – God was just a useful person to bring in to up the *ante*. The IRA, for example, were a Marxist group who were Catholic only in the sense of belonging to an ethnic community. I remember speaking to a group of young men on their way to Ibrox stadium, the home of Glasgow Rangers, bearing a banner stating 'For God and Ulster' (for readers wondering what this has to do with football and Glasgow – don't bother – it's too stupid even to begin to explain). I asked them if they believed in God. 'Don't know – but we're Protestants!' 'Do you go to Church?' 'No (expletive deleted). We go to Ibrox why would we need to go to Church?' Yet doubtless you would cite such political and ethnic Protestantism as another example of religious conflict. Likewise the Sunni and Shia war in Iraq and the conflicts in the former Yugoslavia are primarily ethnic conflicts with religious tribal gods being called in as reinforcements.

And again there is an inconsistency in the atheist argument being used here. On the one hand, you claim that the gods are social constructs of the various tribes/people groups of humanity. On the other you claim that religion is the cause of the various splits and ethnic infighting. Which is it? Do people invent religions so that they can fight one another, or do religions create peoples who will, because of their religion, hate and fight one another? You can't have it both ways – unless you are someone who accepts the Bible's teaching that human beings are inherently selfish and prone towards war, and that they are equally idolatrous, seeking to create 'gods' in their own image – and that the two often come together.

I am grateful to you for your somewhat amusing and sad exposé of the Danish cartoons fiasco. I too have the photo of the Islamic lady with the sign round her neck proudly proclaiming, 'Behead those who say Islam is a violent religion.' And I also deplore the absolute cowardice of the press in Britain who refused to publish the cartoons out of 'respect' and 'sympathy' for the offence and hurt that Muslims suffered. You and I know that the real reason they did not publish was nothing to do with respect and everything to do with fear. *The Independent* newspaper, for example, had no difficulty in publishing the most blasphemous attack upon the Christian God but would not publish these cartoons. The BBC would not show the cartoons but had no difficulty in broadcasting the *Jerry Springer* caricature and assault upon Jesus Christ, thereby showing little 'respect and sympathy' for the hurt and offence that Christians had to put up with. The British media know that there is a core difference between Islam and Christianity: while there may be a few Christians who threaten boycotts or pickets, there are none who are going to seek to kill those who blaspheme our

God, whereas they know full well that any derogatory mention of Mohammed will result in serious death threats and violence. At least you have the grace (and the courage) to acknowledge that Islam is a physical threat, 'on a scale that no other religion has aspired to since the Middle Ages'.

Having said all that I am a little concerned that you use this defence of free speech to justify your caricaturing and ridiculing of religion and in particular Christianity and Christians. It is not that you do not have the right to criticise but rather that with that right also comes responsibility – a responsibility to tell the truth, to listen to others as well, and not to inflame those who might listen to you. The trouble is that your ridicule, combined with an atheist fundamentalism and the bitterness and irrationality of some of your own supporters, leads to persecution and intolerance. The only atheistic states (Stalin's Russia, Mao's China, Pol Pot's Kampuchea and Hitler's Germany) in the world have been the most vicious and cruel that the world has ever seen. Atheistic secular fundamentalism is in my view more intolerant and coercive than almost any religious position.

On the other hand, I would suggest that biblical Christianity is the most tolerant and practical worldview that exists. Why? Because we don't need to impose our views by force (indeed we are forbidden from doing so). We don't need to shut out knowledge because all truth is God's truth. And we don't feel ultimately threatened. We are not interested in political power (or at least we should not be) because we know that our weapons are not the weapons of this world. We respect every human being because they are made in the image of God. Like you, we believe that we should stand up for our views. I am not going to accept Mohammed as a prophet just because some religion tells me to. I must and will, however, respect and love Muslims as fellow human beings in need of God.

And one last thought. One thing that really annoys some atheists is when Christians promise to pray for them. Why do we pray for you? It is not the kind of 'smite the Amalekites' prayer (although sometimes the temptation is enormous!). Rather we pray that God will work in your life, reveal himself to you and draw you to himself. Not so that we can be proved right but rather because it is, believe it or not, the best possible thing that could ever happen to you. Therefore, to pray for you is a supreme act of love because it asks for the best for you. And Jesus tells us that we are to love our enemies. So I do pray for you and for all those who have been deluded into thinking that there is only the material, and that their Creator does not exist. Forgive me.

Yours, etc.

David

LETTER 4 –
THE MYTH OF THE
CRUEL OLD TESTAMENT GOD

Dear Dr Dawkins,

At last we are getting to the meat of your case against God – 'The God Hypothesis'. I wonder in what sense you are using the term 'hypothesis'. Is it that of a supposition? A provisional explanation? Or a theory to be proved or disproved by reference to facts? I suspect that your viewpoint is that mankind, having a 'religious sense' has invented a god or gods to fill in the gaps of our knowledge. In Christian terms this results in Moses, Jesus, Paul, Augustine, Luther, Calvin giving us the 'God hypothesis' to explain what would otherwise be inexplicable. The story then continues – along comes Darwin with another hypothesis and, lo and behold the God hypothesis is disproved. Eureuka! God is a delusion. Humanity has moved onto a higher consciousness and the only thing left to do is write a book which tells people that is the case, and encourages the enlightened to 'come out' and organise politically so that the virus of religion and the old ways can never be used again. The world is saved. Hallelujah!

Except that is not the way it works. And your attack on the 'God Hypothesis' does not work. Not least because in this chapter you really refuse to discuss it. You define the God Hypothesis as, 'there exists a super human, supernatural intelligence who deliberately designed the universe and everything in it, including us' and you tell us that your proof that this is not so is that, 'any creative intelligence of sufficient complexity to design anything, comes into existence only as the end product of an extended process of gradual evolution'. And that is basically it. You spend the remaining 41 pages telling us almost nothing about the God Hypothesis. We learn about secularism and Thomas Jefferson, atheism and American politics, TAP, PAP and NOMA, the Great Prayer Experiment, Little Green Men and why you disagree with Stephen J. Gould, Michael Ruse and other evolutionary appeasers. It is a rambling incoherent chapter, the worst in the book, and is probably the reason that your book has received such a critical slating. *Prospect*, a magazine which largely gives you a sympathetic platform, put it very strongly:

> It has been obvious for years that Richard Dawkins had a fat book on religion in him, but who would have thought him capable of writing one this bad? Incurious, dogmatic, rambling and self-contradictory, it has none of the style or verve of his earlier works.

You begin with a quite vicious and specious attack on the God of the Old Testament. Your first paragraph is one that you enjoy reading to people and it generally gets a round of applause. To me this indicates that you are touching a raw emotional nerve in many of those who hear you. They have a deep-seated hatred of the God of the Bible. I found this paragraph very offensive – so offensive that I will not repeat the whole of it here. Now your standard retort is that you are not offending me, you are offending a god who does not exist. (Cue applause from the fans.) But I'm afraid that you *are* offending me. First, you are implying that I believe in this cruel, capricious and evil god. And second you seem to be working on the basis that as long as you are not directly insulting me, then I cannot be offended. But if you attack my family, my friends, my community I *am* offended because part of my identity is tied up with them. I'm sorry but part of being human is that 'no man is an island' (unless as Nick Hornby points out 'his name is Madagascar'!). My identity is bound up with the God of the Bible and especially Jesus Christ. Therefore, when you attack him you are attacking me. So please don't patronise.

However, I am not a person who believes that the unforgivable sin is to offend. Maybe I deserve the offensive remarks. If what you say is true then they would be deserved. But, your caricature of both the God of the Old Testament and the Jesus of the New is just that – a caricature. Like all such there is an element of truth within it but it is so distorted that it becomes unrecognisable. When I read the Old Testament I find a wonderful God – a God of mercy, justice, beauty, holiness and love, a God who cares passionately for the poor, for his people and for his creation. And, amazingly, it is the same God in the New Testament. I realise that there are difficulties and problems but these are largely caused by your exaggerated caricature. If you take the foundational teachings about God in both the Old and New Testament then you come up with a much more realistic picture.

For example, one of your complaints against God is that he is a jealous God. This is true, but not in the sense of the 'green eyed monster'. God is jealous in the way that a man would expect his wife to be jealous if he started sleeping with other women, or jealous in the way that I am protective of my children. It is about protection, care and honour, not the negative envy. It is difficult to believe that you are not aware of that distinction. My main complaint here is that your description of the God of the Old Testament is not one that the Old Testament itself sets forward. Does this fit with your description?

The Lord works righteousness and justice for all the oppressed. He made known his ways to Moses, his deeds to the people of Israel: The Lord is compassionate and gracious, slow to anger, abounding in love (Psalm 103:6-8).

And there are numerous similar passages. It is only by a very selective citation out of context, ignoring all the passages and teaching about God, that you could come anywhere near the caricature you espouse.

Now of course, as you acknowledge, whether this God is good or bad is irrelevant if he does not exist. Why would we bother arguing about an imaginary being? So that begs the question why you begin the chapter with such a vicious attack upon someone you consider to be an imaginary being? Could it be that it is a cheap shot expressing hatred against a being who might exist? Or that you know the main substance of your argument will appeal to those who have experienced some sort of religious abuse? Is it not the case that you are really aiming at a polemical and emotional response rather than a rational one?

At this point you then go on to discuss polytheism, Oral Roberts, and the Roman Catholic teaching about saints. I am still trying to work out what this has to do with the God Hypothesis. However you do make one point which is now being repeated *ad nauseam* by atheists across the country – that Christians are atheists when it comes to Zeus, Thor and Ra. Atheists just go one god further (cue more gasps of admiration, laughter and cheers). Once again this cheap point fails to take account that there might actually be myths, false gods and delusions. Nor does it recognise that Christians could believe in Christ *because* of the evidence, not in spite of it. Your point has no more validity than a man who announces that a Rolex cannot be real because he once bought a fake watch, or a woman announcing that love does not exist because she once had a bad experience.

It is a rhetorical device that does not actually deal with any of the issues involved.

Another argument that you try to counter is one that I often use. When someone tells me they do not believe in God I often ask them to tell me about the God they do not believe in. They will then come out with the kind of statement that you do at the beginning of the chapter and I will tell them that I do not believe in that God either. You rightly point out that this argument is not valid for someone who is claiming that there is no God whatever his character because there is no supernatural (a faith position, which is of course itself indemonstrable). However, you spend a considerable amount of your book attacking particular versions of God and therefore you open yourself to this rejoinder. Most of us do not believe in the God you so passionately attack. And the *ad hominem* examples you use of eccentric and unbalanced religious people are not what most Christians would identify with. If you stuck to the philosophical debate about whether there was a God at all your book would be a lot shorter (and a lot less popular with your followers). It is your attack on a distorted and perverted version of Christian teaching about God which provides you with the most entertaining smokescreen for your lack of substantial argument on whether God exists in the first place or not.

This leads us on to NOMA ('non overlapping magisteria'). This is the view that science and religion are two separate spheres and that science can neither prove nor disprove the existence of God. The most famous exponent of this view is Stephen J. Gould who in his book *Rocks of Ages: Science and Religion in the Fullness of Life*[9] neatly summarises this as, 'science gets the age of rocks, and religion the rock of ages; science studies how the heavens go, religion how to go to heaven'.

[9] Ballantine Books (1999)

You don't like this. And you certainly don't like theologians. If science cannot answer a question then why bother asking theologians – they are as much use as a chocolate teapot. You write: 'I simply do not believe that Gould could possibly have meant much of what he wrote in *Rock of Ages*.' Are you really suggesting that he is so cowardly that he is prepared to lie in order to have some kind of reconciliation between religion and science? That is a serious charge. And one that is not immediately obvious from reading *Rock of Ages*. I find it a fascinating book with a great deal of valuable insights within it. Take the following for example: 'But I also include among my own scientific colleagues, some militant atheists whose blinkered concept of religion grasps none of the subtlety or diversity.' He also points out that there are people, 'who have dedicated the bulk of their energy, and even their life's definition, to such aggressive advocacy at the extremes that they do not choose to engage in serious and respectful debate.' It's no wonder you don't like him!

However, I would like to take a middle position between your position and that of Mr Gould. He argues for complete separation of the two magisteria (science and religion). You argue for complete annihilation of the religious. I would suggest that there are two magisteria, science and religion which actually do overlap, albeit not totally. There are things that science cannot and possibly never will be able to prove, and there are things that religion does not comment on. Gould's example is correct – the Bible says nothing about the age of rocks and science can tell us nothing about the Rock of Ages – Jesus Christ. However there are places where the two link. For example, if someone claims a miracle that they have been healed from cancer, then science is able to judge whether or not the cancer has gone.

You tell us that the existence of God is a 'scientific hypothesis like any other' and that if God so chose he could reveal himself.

He has. And He will. You tell us that 'even if God's existence is never proved or disproved with certainty one way or the other, available evidence and reasoning may yield an estimate of probability far from 50%'. Really? Why such a confident assertion? Besides which science has moved on since you made that unqualified and unsupported assertion. *The Times* newspaper reported (20 November 2006) that the actual figure was well over 50%.

> The mathematical probability of God's existence is just over 62%. So says a German science magazine. *P.M.* [*Peter Moosleitner's Magazin*] tried to settle the issue by using mathematical formulae devised to determine plausibility and probability. Researchers started with the hypothesis 'God exists', then tried to analyse the evidence in favour or against the hypothesis in five areas: creation, evolution, good, evil and religious experiences. The scientists applied the formulae to calculate how statistically probable different answers were to questions such as 'How probable is it that the evolution of life took place without God?', and 'How probable is it that God created the Universe?' Their conclusion will be cheering to many, although not, perhaps, Richard Dawkins.

Hoisted by your own petard.

By the way, I am fascinated that you think that there is something to be said for treating Buddhism not as a religion but as an ethic or philosophy of life. Would you therefore accept the philosophy that says that handicapped people are born that way because they were bad in a previous life and they are just getting their karma?

Now we move on to the 'Great Prayer Experiment'. This is a complete red herring. By definition the God of the Bible is not mechanical and prayer is communicating with him as a person.

It is only if you accept the slot machine view of prayer (put your prayer in and out will come the answer you want) that any such experiment could be conducted. Given that the Bible does not teach that God is a divine slot machine who answers our prayers mechanically the whole experiment is a nonsense. So I am left once again with asking why you even mentioned it?

Speaking of which what do the position of atheists in the US and your dislike of evolutionary appeasers like Michael Ruse have to do with the God Hypothesis? Do you not think such in-house debates in the Atheist church should be conducted – well, in-house? Or am I right in thinking that your book is actually written as a polemical tract for atheists, a rallying call to political action, rather than a serious discussion about the existence of God? Hence the question in the midst of a chapter meant to be discussing the God Hypothesis, 'What might American atheists achieve if they organised themselves properly?' (p.44).

Before we leave this depressing chapter we have to deal with another tired old argument (put out in almost every atheist forum). When it is pointed out that an atheist cannot disprove God, the standard text book response is now 'yes – no more than we can disprove the Celestial Tea Pot god, the tooth fairy or The Flying Spaghetti Monster'. (I loved the notion of a schism occurring resulting in the *Reformed* Church of the Flying Spaghetti Monster!) Do you seriously think that the evidence for the God of the Bible is on the same level as the tooth fairy? You have not, for example, written a book on the Tooth Fairy Delusion. The evidence for God is on a completely different level. I suspect you know that but again in your rhetorical style the sound-bite put-down works so much better. Let me put it another way – if the only evidence that existed for Jesus Christ was the same as that which exists for the Flying Spaghetti Monster then I and millions of others would not believe in him. So how about dealing with the evidence that we assert and staying away from that which only states your own presupposition – that there is no God?

And finally something on which we can agree: 'A universe in which we are alone except for other slowly evolved intelligences is a very different universe from one with an original guiding agent whose intelligent design is responsible for its very existence.' I live in a universe created by a personal God, the God of mercy, logic, justice, goodness, truth, beauty and love – the God whose purposes and intentions are good. You live in a universe which appeared from nowhere, is going nowhere and means nothing. Perhaps in the next chapter you will give us some reason for this soulless, cold and depressing belief.

Yours, etc.
David

LETTER 5 –
THE MYTH OF THE
SCIENCE/RELIGION CONFLICT

Dear Dr Dawkins,

We are getting closer to your 'proof' that God is a delusion. But before you come on to your 'big argument' you try in this chapter to deal with some of the arguments that theists put forward for the existence of God.

Your understanding of Christian theology is shockingly bad. For example you argue, 'If God is omniscient he already knows how he is going to intervene to change the course of history using his omnipotence – but that means he can't change his mind about his intervention which means he is not omnipotent.' I can hardly believe that a professor at Oxford wrote such a juvenile argument! If you really want to go down that line here are a few more for you. Can God create a stone heavier than he can lift? Can God make a square circle? These may be amusing 'problems' for a teenage class in metaphysics but as a reason for believing that God cannot exist? As Mr McEnroe would say, 'You *cannot* be serious!' A Sunday school teacher once asked the children in her class, 'is there anything that God cannot do?' Not having a particularly good grasp of theology either, she was horrified when a small boy held up his hand and answered 'yes'. She challenged him by asking him what. 'Lie' was the short, succinct and accurate reply. Saying God is omnipotent is not saying that he can do what is immoral or inconsistent with his own nature.

Your discussion of Anselm's Ontological argument is short and largely one with which I would agree. Anselm's view that the greatest thing we can conceive of must exist because otherwise it would not be the greatest thing we could conceive of is a neat philosophical argument but it is only that. However, you spoil your discussion of that with a list of nonsensical satirical 'proofs' from 'godlessgeeks.com' (glad to note that you choose your sources so carefully!) and a vicious attack on the atheist backslider Anthony Flew.

Professor Flew was until recently one of the world's most influential atheists but has apparently had a change of heart and now accepts that there must be a designer. Your attack on him in a footnote in this chapter (and in some of your public speeches) comes across as 'bitchy' – unnecessarily implying that advancing old age must have something to do with his conversion from atheism, that he is not really a great philosopher (contrasted with Bertrand Russell who was a great philosopher and won the Nobel Prize) and that his flawed judgement is shown by his acceptance of the Phillip E. Johnson award for Liberty and Truth. Could you not allow for the possibility that he may have changed his mind? – not because of senility or because that all along he was never really a great philosopher, or because he is seeking the Templeton Prize, but rather because of the evidence and the facts? I guess any atheist who changes his mind needs to know that he will face the wrath of Richard, but please put the claws away. It is very unattractive.

You then deal with three of the major arguments for God – beauty, personal experience and the Bible.

Beauty

You state this argument really badly. For me it is one of the arguments that is central to proving the existence of God. You reduce it to someone asking, 'how do we account for Shakespeare, Schubert or Michelangelo?' But it is much more than that. It is not so much the fact that there is beauty – but why do we as human beings have a sense of beauty? I am sure you will account for that by stating that it is a chemical reaction in our brains caused by millions of years of evolution. But that seems to me at best a partial explanation. Beauty is part of consciousness and it remains one of the great unanswered questions in evolutionary philosophy – where does consciousness come from? When I see the beauty of a sunset over the river Tay, or hear Beethoven's sixth, or walk along the banks of the Mighty Mississippi then I cannot grasp or believe that this is just instinct or impulse that ultimately comes from nowhere. The words of Solomon fit so much better, 'He has made everything beautiful in its time' (Ecclesiastes 3:11).

Is it not a bit of a cheap shot to state that Raphael or Michelangelo only produced their great work because they were paid to? And imply that if they were living today they would be producing the *Evolution Oratorio*. Out of interest where are the great atheist composers, artists, etc? I have no doubt that human beings who are not believers can produce great works of art – but that is because they are *Imago Dei* – created in the image of God. Their creativity is a reflection of the creativity of their creator, whether they acknowledge it or not. The ugliness of much modern art is that it has lost its connection with the divine and the wonder of beauty. Can I suggest that you read Hans Rookmaaker, *Modern Art and the Death of a Culture*[10] for a fascinating and enlightening discussion on this topic? Meanwhile the argument from beauty remains one of the

[10] Apollos (1994)

most powerful arguments for God. The fact that you neither understand nor agree with it hardly constitutes a rational argument against it.

Personal Experience

You also seem to be having enormous difficulty with this argument reducing it to those who hear voices (whether audibly or within their heads) or see visions. You cite one of your 'cleverer' undergraduates who was ordained at least partially because of an experience he had of hearing the devil whilst camping on the Scottish Isles. This was apparently a 'Manx Shearwater' bird. Yet this 'clever' man was stupid enough to see it as a call to the ministry! Which puts him on a level with others you mention – those who have experienced a pink elephant (have you met any such?), the 'Yorkshire Ripper' Peter Sutcliffe hearing Jesus telling him to kill women, President George Bush being 'told by God' to invade Iraq (again what is your source for this information?) and people in asylums thinking they are Napoleon or Charlie Chaplin! According to you the only difference between those locked up in asylums and religious people is that religious people are more numerous. Now, of course there are people who hear voices and see visions which are nothing more than simulations. But does that mean that every such experience is such? I am very wary of people telling me that God has told them something – more often than not they are at the fringes of belief and often do have mental health problems. Nonetheless, I would never be so arrogant as to assume that that is the case for everyone.

Furthermore, you completely misstate the argument from personal experience. The vast majority of Christians do not believe because they have heard a voice or seen a vision – indeed I am struggling to think of anyone I know in that category. Yet personal experience does play a major part (after all it is the experience we know best). C. S. Lewis once wrote that he was a Christian because, 'I arrived where I now am, not by reflection alone, but by reflection on a particular recurrent experience. I am an empirical theist. I have arrived at God by induction.'[11] That is where most Christians are at. We believe because we experience and we think and reflect upon that experience.

There are many other kinds of personal experience which at the very least point us towards God: answered prayer, a sense of God ('truly God is amongst you'), experience of the miraculous, experience of the truths and truthfulness of the Bible and the experience of being filled with the Spirit, to name but a few. From my own experience, I can recall clear, specific and direct answers to prayer, an overwhelming sense of the presence of God, and the Word of God being used to speak to my mind, heart and soul. I am sure you and your followers will manage to diss and explain away all these things and I for one would not argue that I believe in Jesus Christ solely because of any one of them. But the accumulation of these experiences in addition to the truth of the Bible, and the observation of history, creation and society, add up to a very powerful personal apologetic. And not one that can just be dismissed by talking about those who hear voices in their heads. All I have seen teaches me to trust the Creator for all I have not seen.

The Bible

As you also cover this in chapter seven I will resist the temptation to comment too much on what you say in this section. However, there are a couple of points that really do need to be addressed. You begin with a critique of C. S. Lewis' claim that as Jesus claimed to be the Son of God he must have been a Lunatic, a Liar or Lord (Mad, Bad, or God). You write, 'a fourth possibility, almost too obvious to need mentioning, is that Jesus was honestly mistaken'. But that is precisely what Lewis addresses. He makes the point

[11] Cited in C. S. Lewis, *The Authentic Voice*, William Griffin, Lion (1986)

that if Jesus was honestly mistaken in his claim to be the Son of God, it is equivalent to a man who is honestly mistaken in thinking he was a poached egg – it is the lunatic part of the equation. Lewis himself answered this objection when he wrote in 1950: 'The idea of a great moral teacher saying what Christ said is out of the question. In my opinion, the only person who can say that sort of thing is either God or a complete lunatic suffering from the form of delusion which undermines the whole mind of man.' Your book is entitled *The God Delusion*. Lewis presents us with a simple choice. Either you are right and Christians are all deluded people following a deluded Jesus, or the boot is on the other foot and in fact the deluded ones are those who reject Jesus and follow the myths and 'reasons' of the atheist belief system.

You then go on to declare: 'In any case, as I said, there is no good historical evidence that he ever thought he was divine'; which being translated meaneth 'there is no evidence which I have read in *Free Inquiry* or my other atheist "how to" books'. Just what historical evidence have you evaluated? Please note that using *Free Inquiry*, A. N. Wilson and Robin Lane Fox as your sources on biblical material is like me suggesting that those who want to find out about evolution should only go to the *Answers in Genesis* website! The historical evidence for the claims that Jesus made is quite clear. The Gospels make it explicit. And it was after all the reason he was crucified – because he 'blasphemed' by claiming to be God.

You also illustrate the truth of the saying that 'a little learning is a dangerous thing'. For example, you cite as conclusive proof that the gospel of Luke is not historical the fact that a census took place in 6 AD after Herod's death. And yet there is evidence that the census in 6 AD was the second such census and that the first probably took place in 5 BC. The problem is not that there are not significant questions and problems in the Bible (there are). The problem is that you, with all the certainty of the fundamentalist delighting in proving his opponents wrong, seize upon the flimsiest of evidence and, without any further investigation, make sweeping statements that this proves the Bible wrong.

In this regard I am astounded at how out of touch you are with modern biblical scholarship. You write: 'Ever since the 19th century scholarly theologians have made an overwhelming case that the gospels are not reliable accounts of what happened in the history of the real world.' Unless you are adopting the phrase 'scholarly theologians' as a euphemism for 'those who happen to agree with me' your statement is just plainly and demonstrably false. Can I suggest that you ask your Oxford colleague Alister McGrath, Principal of Wycliffe Hall, why he is ignoring this overwhelming case? Perhaps you should read his *Christian Theology: An Introduction*?[12] I am sure it would be enormously helpful and prevent you making the kind of gaffes that you pour out here.

Your position reminds me of a debate that was held in the Dundee Contemporary Arts Centre concerning the *Da Vinci Code*.[13] During the course of the evening the most heated opposition came from a couple of people who made the same claim that scholars no longer accepted the Gospels as historical accounts. When one man was challenged on this and told that he was being 'so 20th century' (although he was in actual fact being so 19th century) he struggled to name one modern scholar who took that position. Eventually, he came up with the name Bultmann, whose main work was done in the first half of the 20th century. On the other hand I can think of at least 20 major biblical scholars at 'real' Universities today (not Mickey Mouse tin hut Bible colleges) who would argue for the basic historicity

[12] Blackwell (1993)
[13] Corgi (2004)

of the Gospels. At the very least, any statement which claims the scholarly position is that the historical evidence for the Bible is the same as that for the *Da Vinci Code*, is at best ignorant and at worst downright deceitful. Indeed it is so breathtaking in its audacity that it reminds me of Goebbels' maxim that the bigger the lie (and the more it is stated with absolute conviction) the more people are likely to believe it.

Religious Scientists

You also attribute a somewhat strange argument to theists: 'The Argument from Admired Religious Scientists'. I say 'strange' because I have never heard anyone say that they believed in God because such and such a scientist believes. However, what we do say is that the atheist attempt to set science against religion is one that is fatally undermined by the considerable number of scientists who are also believers. And I guess that is what bothers you and why you are so disparaging about the ones you identify. You neatly dismiss all pre-Darwinian scientists by claiming that it was normal for people to profess belief and that they would come under pressure if they did not. Indeed such is your disdain for your fellow scientists who are believers that you even hint that those who continue to profess faith may be doing so because of social or economic factors. Furthermore, you state that they are so rare that 'they are a subject of amused bafflement to their peers in the academic community'. So Asa Gray (American Botanist), Charles D. Walcott (discoverer of Burgess Shale fossils), T. Dobzhansky (Russian Orthodox evolutionary biologist), R. J. Berry (Professor of Genetics at University College London), Owen Gingerich (Professor of Astronomy and History of Science at Harvard) and Francis Collins (Head of the Human Genome Project) are all 'sources of amused bafflement'? I think nothing illustrates your arrogance and almost pathological hatred of God and religion more than this dismissive, patronising and 'who's not for us is against us' view of your scientific colleagues.

Incidentally, I noted with interest your footnote contrasting the 'administrative' head of the American branch of the Human Genome Project with 'the brilliant and non religious buccaneer' of science, Craig Venter. It is an interesting contrast, not least because of the descriptive language you employ. But what fascinates me most is the different way that the different worldviews impacted how they wanted to use their science. Whereas Francis Collins, the Christian, wanted to keep the Human Genome Project in the public domain and the information available and accessible to all, your 'brilliant and non religious buccaneer' wanted to privatise the whole project to make money. His company, Celera, aimed to file patents on many of the genes and, had they been successful, would have only allowed the data to be available to those who paid large sums of money. I think that is an apt metaphor for the difference between two very different worldviews. On the one hand there is an alliance of science with those who seek to use it for the public good of all (and not just private profit), who recognise its limits and who believe that they are accountable to God for what they do with his gifts. On the other there is an alliance of science with a godless morality and materialism which seeks to use knowledge for personal gain and private profit. I think we have been down this scientific materialistic route before – I believe that Stalin, Mao and Hitler all thought that their societies should be governed with such 'science' and morality. I am sorry if that offends you and I am not trying to equate your 'nice' atheism with the nasty but I honestly believe that this is where your atheistic hatred of God will eventually lead society. Indeed, it is one of the reasons that I believe in the God of the Bible – because without that biblical worldview I have no real explanation of, nor defence against, the evil of which humans are capable.

Let me finish by pointing out that you missed out the most important argument of all for the existence of God – the person and work of Jesus Christ. By far the number one reason I believe and trust God is because of Jesus Christ.

In the past God spoke to our forefathers through the prophets at many times and in various ways, but in these last days he has spoken to us by his Son, whom he appointed heir of all things, and through whom he made the universe. The Son is the radiance of God's glory and the exact representation of his being, sustaining all things by his powerful word (Hebrews 1:1-3).

The presence, power and perfection of Jesus Christ is no delusion.

Yours, etc.
David

LETTER 6 –
THE MYTH OF THE CREATED GOD AND THE UNCREATED UNIVERSE

Dear Dr Dawkins,

Finally we arrive at the centre of your book and its main argument. The title of your fourth chapter is a bold claim: 'Why there almost certainly is no God'. In it you propose to prove, insofar as it is possible, that there is no God. I found this chapter astonishing. Allow me to explain why. I had expected that your case against God was to be a cumulative one – a bit like your view of evolution. Faced with the mountain of Divinity and the universal belief of humankind in a God or gods, I expected you to climb Mount Improbable gradually, building a case slowly and leading us by a cumulative process to the view that there is no God. However you go for the big leap. You think you have the killer argument and you can go straight to the Holy Grail of atheism and then have a gentle slide downhill afterwards, picking off the remaining theistic arguments because you have already proved there is no God.

What is this killer argument? The one that even Nietzsche could not find? Your argument goes like this. Evolution is true. Evolution explains the illusion of design. The design argument is the main argument for God. Therefore there is no God. And the reason that the design argument does not work? The point that you think almost 'certainly' proves there is no God? The core and heart of your intellectual justification for your emotional atheism? It is astounding. (I almost feel at this point that there should be a drum roll...) The argument is: 'Who designed the Designer?'

In your own words:

> Once again, this is because the designer himself (herself/itself) immediately raises the problem of his own origin.

> Indeed design is not a real alternative at all because it raises an even bigger problem than it solves: who designed the designer?

> But whatever else we may say, design certainly does not work as an explanation for life, because design is ultimately not cumulative.

> As ever the theist's answer is deeply unsatisfying because it leaves the existence of God unexplained.

> To suggest that the original prime mover was complicated enough to indulge in intelligent design, to say nothing of mind reading millions of humans simultaneously, is tantamount to dealing yourself a perfect hand at bridge.

It is clear that this point is very important to you and the foundation of the rest of your arguments. When I read it I was genuinely shocked. Not because of its originality, killer force or overwhelming logic, but rather because of its banality. 'Who made God?' is a question I would expect from a six-year-old. 'Who made God then?' is the accusation I would expect from a sixteen-year-old. I am genuinely surprised to find the world's most famous atheist (now that the philosopher Antony Flew[14]

---

[14] Life-long atheist philosopher Anthony Flew recently announced that he was persuaded by evidence of intelligent design that there was a supreme being. His conversion was to Deism not necessarily to Theism.

has defected) and an Oxford Professor to boot, using it as *the* intellectual foundation for his atheism. This is the argument that is going to change the world? This is the key?! Forgive my incredulity and perhaps even the slight mocking tone but you are very quick to mock some of the stupider theistic arguments. Using the 'Who made God?' argument is the atheist equivalent of the argument from degree.

The answer to the question who made God is simply 'nobody'. God is not made. God is the Creator, not the creation. God is outside of time and space. (This is not to say that he is not also in time and space and that there is not plenty evidence for him there.) God creates *ex nihilo*. That's what makes him God. He does not craft from what is already there. He creates time, space and matter from nothing. I realise for you that is nonsense because the core of your creed is that evolution means that everything starts from the simple and becomes more complex, therefore because that is the case (and any designer would have to be incredibly complex) God cannot exist. But even if we grant that this is true for biology, biology is not everything. As Joe Fitzpatrick argues, 'Dawkins is methodologically confused, taking a principle of biological science and making it into a universal principle.'[15] To argue as you do is to take an incredible leap of faith and to beg the question. Who says that everything, including God himself, has to come from something? Christians and other theists do not argue that God was created. That is precisely the point. He did not come from anywhere. He has always been. He did not evolve, nor was he made. If there is a personal Creator of the Universe then it makes perfect sense to regard him as complex, beyond our understanding and eternal. When you state that you can disprove God because there can *de facto* never be anything that was uncreated you are engaging in a circular argument. We do not believe in a created God. We believe in an uncreated

[15] In the Catholic Magazine *Open House*, (January 2007)

supernatural power. I'm afraid you disprove nothing when you argue against the existence of a created God.

Let us assume for the moment that evolution is true, why would that disprove God? Let us assume that the Intelligent Design movement is wrong – why would that disprove God? It would disprove one argument that some theists use but there are many other arguments. Moreover, there are many Christians who do not accept the ID science and who continue to be believers in the God of the Bible. You mention with particular praise Kenneth Miller, of Brown University and author of *Finding Darwin's God*.[16] He strongly disagrees with Michael Behe, one of the leading ID scientists, and with the whole ID movement. By your logic he should then be an atheist. He is not. He is a theist. I am sure you would not call him stupid but you do accuse other theists who are also 'good' scientists of 'compartmentalising'. To my mind this is patronising and the equivalent of accusing them of a fundamental dishonesty. To you, they have the evidence to prove there is no God (who designed the designer?) but they do not have the moral courage or the mental capacity to embrace the logical conclusions. Except of course these conclusions are not logical. As McGrath puts it, 'There is a substantial logical gap between Darwinism and atheism, which Dawkins seems to prefer to bridge by rhetoric rather than evidence.'[17]

In order for there to be natural selection there has to be something to select. Where did that come from? This is where Aquinas' 'theistic proofs' – the Unmoved Mover, the Uncaused Cause and the Cosmological arguments – come into their own. In terms of the origin of matter there are only three alternatives:

1. Something came from nothing. At one point there was no universe, there was no material, there was no matter, no

[16] HarperCollins (2000)
[17] *Dawkins' God,* Blackwell (2004) p. 87

time, no space. And out of that big nothing there came the Big Bang and our vast universe, tiny planet, evolution and the human species. Such a notion is beyond the realms of reason and is a total nonsensical fantasy.

2. Something was eternal. In other words matter has always existed. There is a lump of rock, or a mass of gas or some kind of matter which had no beginning and will probably have no end. And at some point that matter exploded and we ended up with the finely tuned and wonderful universe we now inhabit.

3. Something was created – *ex nihilo* – out of nothing. And that Creator has to be incredibly powerful, intelligent and awesome beyond our imagination.

I cannot see any other logical alternative. Can you? I found it fascinating that when you were challenged about this you argued that we don't know where matter came from but one day scientists will find out. Despite this rather touching faith in the potential omniscience of scientists, I'm afraid that will not do. The existence of God is not dependent on the argument from design as regards evolution; it *is* dependent on the fact that there is any matter at all, and that we live in a universe which is so finely tuned that life is possible at all. Why is there something rather than nothing? And why does that something manage to produce you and me? That is not a question which you can just brush aside or express no interest in.

Let's move on to this second stage. It is not only the fact that matter exists at all, but that it is so ordered that life can exist. As a young boy I was brought up in an area which had very little light pollution and so during the winter nights I often walked under the stars, risking injury by continually gazing upwards. The stars awe, amaze and fascinate me. Nowadays I can visit the local observatory in Dundee where I am greeted by an inscription above the door: 'This observatory is given that you may observe the wonders of the Creator in the heavens.' Above the door of the 'old' Cavendish Laboratories in Cambridge – where J. J. Thompson discovered the electron and Crick and Watson determined the structure of DNA – there is an inscription: 'Magna opera Domini exquisita in omnes voluntates ejus' (Great are the works of the Lord; they are pondered by all who delight in them, Psalm 111:2). This theology does not seem to have hampered the sciences in Cambridge, which has still managed to produce more Nobel prize winners in science than any other institution, including Oxford – 29 Nobel prizes in Physics, 22 in Medicine and 19 in Chemistry!

To stare at the stars is for me one of the major if not *the* major reason for believing in God. I found it difficult to believe that this vast universe existed by itself, or as the result of an accident. As I have grown in years and in knowledge, it has been a real delight to discover that my natural instincts in observation are in accord with what science has also discovered. Whereas I struggle with most books on evolution because of a lack of knowledge (your books have actually been the most accessible and interesting), I really enjoy cosmology. Recently I have been reading Owen Gingerich's *God's Universe* and Francis Collins, *The Language of God* which beautifully explain why the Universe is the best evidence for the existence of God. After going into detail about the wonders of the Big Bang, Collins cites with approval the astrophysicist Robert Jastrow from *God and the Astronomers*:[18] 'For the scientist who has lived by his faith in the power of reason, the story ends like a bad dream. He has scaled the mountain of ignorance; he is about to conquer the highest peak; as he pulls himself over the final rock, he is greeted by a band of theologians who have been sitting there for centuries.' I thought you would like that!

[18] W. W. Norton (2000)

Jastrow also writes, 'Now we see how the astronomical evidence leads to a biblical view of the origin of the world. The details differ, but the essential elements and the astronomical and biblical accounts of Genesis are the same; the chain of events leading to man commenced suddenly and sharply at a definite moment in time, in a flash of light and energy.' Stephen Hawking points out that if the rate of expansion one second after the Big Bang had been smaller by even one part in ten thousand million million, the universe would have recollapsed before it ever reached its present state. If it had been greater by one part in a million then the stars and planets would not have been able to form. Is that not spine-chillingly incredible? Constants like the speed of light, the force of gravity and electromagnetism all need to work precisely together for there to be life. Apparently there are fifteen such constants. Wonderful and incredible.

If you hold the position that matter is eternal, which you must as a rationalistic atheist, then you are left with this vast improbability of the fine-tuning of the Universe. And it is an improbability that cannot be explained by evolution because there is nothing to evolve. The question is how did we get the conditions for evolution? I guess you could argue that we were very, very, very lucky – to the point of one in ten thousand million million. That takes an enormous amount of faith. Like the example you cite from the philosopher, John Leslie, who talks about a man sentenced to death standing in front of a firing squad of ten expert marksmen. All of them miss. There could be some way of explaining such 'good fortune', but it is such an improbable event. Multiply that a million times and you have the improbability of the universe as we have it. So, in order to avoid that, what can you do? Well you can invent the multiverse, the view that there are billions of universes co-existing like bubbles of foam and the chances are that at least one will end up with some form of life. You even cite Lee Smolin's view that daughter universes are born from parent universes and that they in effect evolve thus eventually getting to a stage where life is possible. This is really special pleading and indicates desperation to try and explain the universe we have without God.

You keep telling us that science is about what we can observe, that it is about fact and empirical evidence. The multiverse notion is a 'sci-fi' nonsense for which there is no evidence whatsoever. One almost gets the impression that you would accept any theory as long as it did not involve the possibility of there being a God! This becomes especially evident when we move on to the last chapter – there you take this speculation even further citing David Deutsch's *The Fabric of Reality: Towards a Theory of Everything*.[19] Deutsch speculates that there is a vast and rapidly growing number of universes, existing in parallel and mutually undetectable – except through the porthole of quantum mechanical experiments. You write, 'In some of these universes I am already dead. In a small minority of them, you have a green moustache.' And you have the nerve to mock those of us who believe that the Creator of the Universe could raise the dead! Are you really so desperate to escape God that you have to have faith in a universe where there are green moustaches? Why stop there? Why not suggest that the Wachowski brothers' film *The Matrix* is correct? The world we live in is not really real – we only think it is because we are wired up to a giant computer which feeds our minds with the illusion of reality. Maybe there is some giant computer program somewhere that is feeding our mind with the illusion that we are really reading this?!

You like to suggest that your position is a logical one caused by the fact that Darwin has raised your own consciousness and you seem to think that those who do not agree with you are not so highly evolved (at least in consciousness). Your position is *the* scientific one and you set up the debate so that it is always

[19] Penguin Books Ltd (1998)

the forces of reason and science against the blind irrationality of faith. I'm afraid that that just does not square with the facts. In fact, although you state that science is the reason you do not believe in God you offer no substantive scientific reasons as to why we should not believe in God. Your arguments for atheism as a belief system are primarily arguments which are non-scientific. And you need to stop misrepresenting those of us who believe in God as doing so because we are looking for a 'God of the gaps' – someone who will fill in until 'science' gives us the real answer. The reason that we believe in God is *because* of the evidence, *because* of science (knowledge), *because* of what we see in the universe. As Francis Collins declares, 'There are good reasons to believe in God, including the existence of mathematical principles and order in creation. They are positive reasons, based on knowledge, rather than default assumptions based on a temporary lack of knowledge.'[20] I'd take the awe of understanding over the awe of ignorance any day.

Let me leave you with a couple of other quotes:

> The best data we have are exactly what I would have predicted, had I nothing to go on but the five books of Moses, the Psalms, the Bible as a whole. (Arno Penzias, the Nobel-prize-winning scientist who discovered background radiation that proved the Big Bang.[21])

> It would be very difficult to explain why the universe should have begun in just this way, except as the act of a God who intended to create beings like us. (Stephen Hawking, *A Brief History of Time*.)

---

[20] *The Language of God*, p. 93

[21] Malcolm Browne, 'Clues to the Universe's Origin Expected', *New York Times*, Mar. 12, 1978, p. 1, col. 54, cited in Jerry Bergman, 'Arno A. Penzias: Astrophysicist, Nobel Laureate', http://www.asa3.org/ASA/PSCF/1994/PSCF9-94Bergman.html

I am personally persuaded that a super intelligent Creator exists beyond and within the cosmos, and that the rich context of congeniality shown by our universe, permitting and encouraging the existence of self-conscious life, is part of the Creator's design and purpose. (Owen Gingerich, *God's Universe*.)

… the extreme difficulty, or rather the impossibility, of conceiving this immense and wonderful universe, including man with his capacity for looking far backwards and far into futurity, as the result of blind chance or necessity. When thus reflecting I feel compelled to look to a First Cause having an intelligent mind in some degree analogous to that of man; and I deserve to be called a Theist. (Charles Darwin, cited in the book you mention – Brown's *Finding Darwin's God*.)

In bringing up the argument of the origin of matter and of the universe you have in fact scored an enormous own goal. Instead of proving that there almost certainly is no God, you have demonstrated that there almost certainly is. It might be a good idea to find out who he is, stop burying your head in the sand and stop shaking your fist at a God you say cannot exist because in order to exist he would have to be more complex than you. He is.

Yours, etc.
David

P.S. – there is much in this chapter that I have not interacted with including another attack on the Templeton Foundation and further criticism of another backsliding, compromising scientist – Freeman Dyson. But there are a couple of quotes that I cannot resist. First, you point out that, 'It is utterly illogical to demand complete documentation of every step of every narrative, whether in evolution or any other science.' I agree. Can I suggest that you also apply that to theology and the Bible? Why do you demand that we have to have evidence and documentation for every detail of every event described in the Bible? Of course we are aware that there are 'gaps', but why do you demand that unless we fill them and give you 'the complete picture', then what we have must be classed as false?

Second, you declare, 'When pressed, many educated Christians today are too loyal to deny the virgin birth and the resurrection. But it embarrasses them because their rational minds know it is absurd, so they would much rather not be asked.' Wrong. An educated Christian believes in the God of the Bible who created this whole amazing universe. To raise the dead or create a virgin birth seems to me to be, if not quite chickenfeed in comparison, at least very probable and doable and certainly not illogical. Besides which, I would regard it as a whole lot more logical to believe that an eternal omnipotent God could raise the dead, than to believe that the explanation for our universe involves there being multi-universes in which I exist or am already dead – with or without my green moustache!

LETTER 7 –
THE MYTH OF THE
INHERENT EVIL OF RELIGION

Dear Dr Dawkins,

There is an English nursery rhyme – *The Grand Old Duke of York*. You know how it goes

> *The Grand Old Duke of York*
> *He had ten thousand men;*
> *He marched them up to the top of the hill;*
> *And he marched them down again.*

I kind of feel that this is where we have now arrived. You have led us up to the top of the hill to prove why there is no God. Having in my opinion failed, in the rest of your book you now march us back down again, having a swipe at your favourite religious targets on the way. Chapter five on the roots of religion is your attempt to answer why religion is so prevalent in every society throughout the world. 'Though the details differ across the world, no known culture lacks some version of the time-consuming, wealth-consuming, hostility-provoking rituals, the anti-factual counter productive fantasies of religion.' Chapter eight follows up on the title of your Channel Four TV series, 'The Root of all Evil?' I find your analysis in these two chapters hard to respond to because they depend upon the failed thesis that

God has been proven not to exist and, because your treatment of religion is imbalanced, distorted and reflective, not so much of objective analysis but rather your own subjective anti-God feelings.

There have been numerous attempts to explain why religion is so prevalent. Some neuroscientists have argued that there is a 'god centre' in the brain; some psychiatrists argue for the placebo effect of religion whereby people are comforted and have their stress reduced; Marxists argue for the view that religion is a tool of the ruling class to subjugate their people; and Freudians will argue that religion is part of the same irrational mechanism in the brain that makes us fall in love. That latter point reminds me of studying, as a student at the University of Edinburgh, E. P. Thompson's *The Making of the English Working Class*,[22] in which he explains away the Methodist revival by suggesting it was an expression of repressed sexuality. Even then I found it a forced and somewhat amusing explanation.

Your own preference is to suggest that religion is a misfiring by-product of natural selection. Somehow, we have developed a survival mechanism which means that we tend to be obedient to our ancestors. Children naturally have trusting obedience which, whilst it is good for survival, makes them very gullible to 'mind viruses' such as religion. This is where another of your pet theories comes to the fore – the notion of memes. This is an attempt to link Darwinian evolution with the development of ideas. As regards religion, it means, as McGrath points out, 'people do not believe in God because they have given long and careful thought to the matter; they do so because they have been infected by a powerful meme.'[23] But this idea falls down on at least three levels. First, there is no empirical evidence of such a theory – this is once again a 'science of the gaps' just making

[22] Gollancz (1963)
[23] Cited in McGrath, *Dawkins' God*.

things up as you go along in order to fit everything into your all-encompassing evolutionary theory. Second, if it were true then your own ideas, including Darwinian evolution, would be considered memes as well. Third, as Simon Conway Morris, Professor of Evolutionary Paleobiology at the University of Cambridge, points out, 'Memes are trivial, to be banished by simple mental exercises. In any wider context, they are hopelessly, if not hilariously, simplistic.'[24] And I would go way beyond that. They are dangerous. If you regard religion as a virus what should be done with a virus? It should be eradicated.

Which leads me to jump to chapter eight – 'What's Wrong with Religion?' You state that you do not like confrontation and that you 'regularly refuse invitations to take part in formal debates'. I'm afraid this will not wash. Your book is highly confrontational. You surround yourself with those who agree with you before being aggressive about those who do not. In fact, you set up debates and this chapter with a basic myth/ meme that is a largely influential one in our culture today. It is the view that religion is essentially something evil and that atheism by contrast is good. Whilst it would only be a fool who denies the fact that some aspects of religion and some religious people have caused a great deal of harm in the world, it is equally foolish to make the kind of irresponsible sweeping statements that you do here – in order to foster the myth that religion is in essence harmful. This is an atheist half-truth which is erroneously but widely accepted. The *Guardian* newspaper in December 2006 carried a survey of British people, which made clear that a majority of people thought religion was harmful and divisive. Of course all religions were lumped together as one. It is the equivalent of the doctrine of the axis of evil – the world

[24] From Simon Morris, *Life's Solution: Inevitable Humans in a Lonely Universe*, Cambridge University Press (2003)

is divided into the good guys and the bad guys. You share that simplistic, fundamentalist view.

But you don't like being called a fundamentalist. A fundamentalist is someone by your definition who believes 'in a holy book'. A fundamentalist would never change their mind: 'we believe in evolution because the evidence supports it, and we would abandon it overnight if new evidence arose to disprove it. No real fundamentalist would ever say anything like that.' Really? I believe that the Bible is true. I believe that Jesus rose from the dead. I believe that God is the Creator of heaven and earth. I believe that all human beings are created equally in his image. And I would abandon these beliefs tomorrow if new evidence arose to disprove them.

I think there are several reasons why you are called a fundamentalist. First, you are passionate about what you believe. Anyone who is passionate about what they believe is often labelled a fundamentalist. Now of course you argue that the hostility you 'occasionally voice towards religion is limited to words'. You are not going to bomb anyone or behead anyone or fly planes into skyscrapers. But on page 318 you directly contradict yourself when commenting on the old adage 'Sticks and stones may break my bones, but words can never hurt me.' You declare, 'the adage is true as long as you don't really believe the words'. What's sauce for the goose is sauce for the gander.

If you are concerned about the impact that words used by religious people may have then you must apply the same criteria to yourself. When you go around describing religion as evil and as a virus you should not be surprised if there are those who hear your words and put them into practice in a way you would not like. Nice middle-class Professors from Oxford do not kill (unless you watch Inspector Morse) but then neither did nice middle class Professors from Nuremberg in the 1930s. Atheists don't bomb or burn? Try telling that to the members of the

77 churches in Norway which were burnt down when some over-zealous young atheists took on board the teaching about how dangerous and evil religion was. Clearly you have also forgotten the clarion calls of some of the great atheist thinkers of the recent past. Bakunin and Lenin for example both argued that religion was a virus which needed to be eradicated – they both advocated and implemented the killing of believers as a social obligation. In this they were only developing the philosophy of Nietzsche:

> I call Christianity the one great curse, the one great intrinsic depravity, the one great instinct for revenge for which no expedient is sufficiently poisonous, secret, subterranean, petty – I call it the one immortal blemish of mankind....

Another atheist writer in advocating attacks on those who believe in the Judaeo-Christian God writes:

> Any intelligent Antichrist methodology at that point will involve a consolidation of strength, public education in the ways of science and logic for our individual members, and actions taken against the remaining believers. The new society must first stabilize itself and come to a point of economic self-sufficiency and growth in social, intellectual, economic, technological and cultural areas. Once this is achieved, the executions of diehard Christians and Jews should bother no one. (Taken from the 'Church Arson' website.)

Of course, it would be entirely wrong to take the actions and words of a handful of atheist extremists as being indicative of atheists in general (just as it is wrong of you to take the actions and words of a handful of 'Christian' extremists as indicative of Christians) but please bear in mind that your vehemence and language can have consequences that are as serious as the consequences of the vehemence and language of some 'religious' fundamentalists.

Second, you do not debate – which gives the impression that you know you are right and that there is nothing really to discuss. It also reinforces the impression that you operate within a very closed worldview. In this sense your website has more fundamentalist believers than many religious ones I know. Another sense in which you can be described as fundamentalist is the way that you attack anyone who dares to disagree with you and how you gleefully jump upon books that support your point of view. An example of this is when you hammered Mother Teresa as a woman with 'cock-eyed judgement' not worthy of a Nobel Prize and 'sanctimoniously hypocritical', on the basis of one hostile book you read.

Third, you caricature, mock and misrepresent those who disagree with you. This is easy to do when you do not debate with them but it is not fair. As C. S. Lewis pointed out, 'Such people put up a version of Christianity suitable for a child of six and make that the object of their attack.'[25]

Chapter eight for example is full of the worst examples of this kind of 'reasoning'. You cite the case of Abdul Rahman who was sentenced to death because he converted to Christianity. And this in the modern liberated Afghanistan we have set up, and that our soldiers are currently dying to defend. Then you equate the Afghan Taliban with 'the American Taliban'. This is disingenuous and dishonest. Whilst there are many aspects of the association between right-wing politics and some evangelicalism in the US which I cannot stand, it is clearly wrong to compare them with the Taliban in Afghanistan. No-one (even from the extremes) is calling for the State to execute those who convert to another religion, no-one is arguing for women to be

[25] C. S. Lewis, *Mere Christianity* (1952)

banned from education or that all American women should be covered up. To the ignorant, the link between the Taliban and Christianity is a neat tie up and a further justification for their opposition to Christianity. But that is only to the ignorant. You are not ignorant and you know this.

Another example you use of extremism is Pastor Fred Phelps of Westboro Baptist Church, of 'God Hates Fags' infamy. 'It is easy to write Fred Phelps off as a nut, but he has plenty support from people and their money.' You even cite as evidence for this the fact that since 1991 he has been able to organise one demonstration every four days. Is the fact that one self-publicising head-banger manages to organise a handful of people every four days to carry obnoxious banners proof that religion is dangerous? Are you really blaming Mother Teresa, the Pope, Billy Graham, one thousand million Christians throughout the world and even 'yours truly' for every lunatic who expresses their mental and emotional imbalance in religious terms? That is as rational as my suggesting that because Dr Josef Mengele was a scientist, all scientists are to blame and therefore science should be banned. The point is simply that anyone could produce a list of fringe mentally imbalanced people on any subject. That does not invalidate the subject.

You have a good reason for equating Christianity with the unbalanced fringe. It suits your purpose to agree with them as to what Christianity is. That's why you interview extremists. You set up straw men and then it makes you look so much more reasonable. But that is the tactic of the fundamentalist who is out to prove that he alone has the truth, rather than the scholar or the seeker after truth. A number of years ago I went to a meeting where the speaker was a theonomist, the late Greg Bahnsen. The majority of what he said was excellent but then he made a quantum leap trying to prove that the Old Testament Mosaic civil code, including the punishments, should be applied by the state today. I, like most of the Christians there, was horrified at his misapplication of the Bible. But there was a group of people there who supported him and agreed with his interpretation of the Bible – the people from the Secular Humanist society. You need religious extremists to prove your point and they need you. It's a kind of mutual fundamentalist admiration society where both of you justify your extremism by citing the opposition. A plague on both your houses.

You know this so you attempt to justify the link by pointing out that, 'even mild and moderate religion helps to provide the climate of faith in which extremism naturally flourishes'. Do you think that it would be fair of me to point out that even mild and moderate anti-religious rhetoric helps to provide the climate of hatred and certainty in which extremism naturally flourishes? Again, you can only get away with this by using your own definition of faith and refusing to acknowledge the good that is done by religious people because of their religion. You define faith as believing something without evidence – a definition which is just something that you have made up in your own head and has nothing to do with Christianity. My faith is based on evidence. The minute you disprove that evidence I will change my faith. But although you lump together all faiths and all faith as the same, for polemical and political reasons, you are actually creating a grave danger.

Take the question of Christianity and Islam. It suits you to lump them both together (including the extremists). Patrick Sookhdeo's article, *The Myth of Islamic Tolerance*,[26] which you cite, is an excellent discussion of the differences between Christian theology and Islamic theology. The danger is that in your equating Christianity and Islam (because of the wilful blindness caused by your hatred of religion *per se*) you would end up handing Islam a victory – at least in Europe. Secularism

[26] The *Spectator* (30 July 2005)

cannot handle nor deal with Islam – it does not have the spiritual, moral or intellectual fibre to do so. If you were to destroy Christianity (which is your aim), what that would leave is a spiritual and moral vacuum in Western Europe that would be filled by either a new fascism or Islam. Then you would find out for real the fact that all religions are not the same.

Despite all the above it is still a truism for many that 'religious' necessarily means 'evil' and is seen as the cause of division. I would suggest that, as so often is the case, the reality of the situation is more complex. Miroslav Volf, in his work *Exclusion and Embrace: Theological Exploration of Identity, Otherness and Reconciliation*,[27] examines the complex ways in which human beings tyrannise one another and the subtle way in which religion is subverted by the human desire to define the self against the other. In other words the problem is not that human beings are basically good and that religion turns them bad, but rather that human beings will use anything, including religion, to justify their own selfish behaviour.

Before finishing, let's return to the question of where religion comes from. Why are people so religious? As you point out, evolutionary psychologist Paul Bloom tells us that we are naturally dualists believing that there is a difference between mind and matter. Bloom even suggests that we are innately predisposed to be creationists. Dorothy Kelman points out that children are intuitive theists. I would actually agree with this and respectively suggest that this evidence contradicts another atheist myth – that people are only religious because they have been brainwashed as children. In actual fact, the default position for humans is to be religious. It takes the 'education' of secularists to get them to a 'higher consciousness' (in other words to disbelieve what they would naturally believe).

[27] Abingdon Press, USA (1994)

Can I make a tentative suggestion to you? That the reason why human beings worship is that there is someone to worship? That the reason we have a sense of God (as opposed to other animals – when did you last see rabbits holding a prayer meeting or cows a worship service?) is because God has given us that sense? That the reason we are spiritual is because we have a spirit? As C. S. Lewis argued, 'Creatures are not born with desires unless satisfaction for those desires exists. A baby feels hunger: well, there is such a thing as food. A duckling wants to swim: well, there is such a thing as water. Men feel sexual desire: well, there is such a thing as sex. If I find in myself a desire which no experience in this world can satisfy, the most probable explanation is that I was made for another world.'

You cite the following in your attack upon those of us who are deluded by our belief in God: 'Self deception is hiding the truth from the conscious mind the better to hide if from others.... There is a tendency for humans consciously to see what they wish to see.' Perhaps the boot is on the other foot. What if there is an Atheist Delusion – where we delude ourselves that our natural God consciousness within is not real? That the evidence is not really evidence at all? And that God does therefore not exist? Would not the Psalmist's description be right? 'The Fool has said in his heart, there is no God' (Psalm 14:1).

Yours, etc.
David

LETTER 8 –
THE MYTH OF GODLESS MORALITY

Dear Dr Dawkins,

As a young boy I watched with fascination *The World at War* on our TV screens (the whole series is now available on DVD and is regularly repeated on the History Channel). One scene in particular has stuck in my mind. A group of French Jewish men, women and children were herded into a large barn by Nazi soldiers. The barn was set on fire and the Jews were given a simple choice – they could come out of the barn and be shot or they could stay in and be burnt to death. It horrified me then and it horrifies me now. In fact, it so disturbed me that when I took the opportunity to do Sixth Year Studies at school, I determined to look at Weimar Germany and then went on to study history at the University of Edinburgh in order to try and answer the question, 'why?' The same question that was displayed on the poster hanging in my bed-sit, superimposed over the soldier being shot in the back and the young naked girl running across a bridge screaming as napalm burned into her flesh. This question of morality is thus of great importance – not only for me but I suspect for most people.

You address this issue of morality in chapter six and in particular the question as to why we are good. As far as I can understand it, your case seems to be as follows: you define goodness as altruism and therefore point out that we tend to be altruistic towards those of our own kin because we are genetically programmed to care for those who are most likely to have copies of the same genes that are in us. In addition to this there is reciprocal altruism – the 'you scratch my back and I'll scratch yours' theory. Kinship and reciprocal altruism are the twin pillars on which a Darwinian explanation of morality is based. To these you add reputation (we want to be seen to be 'good') and then the notion that altruistic giving may be seen as a form of superiority – a way of buying self-advertising. You also explain 'kindness' or 'sympathy' as a blessed Darwinian mistake. And that's it. That is the Darwinian explanation of morality. There are so many problems with this approach.

First, it does not seem much of a morality. It is still primarily focused on the Selfish Gene. It is all about me, me and mine. As a Christian I believe that the Bible teaches that human beings *are* fundamentally selfish and self-centred – however the Bible is not content to leave us there. There is something better. Christ came to challenge and to deliver us from the self-centredness which you glorify as the basis of morality.

Second, it is deterministic. There is no concept of free will, choice or responsibility. We are only 'good' because we are programmed to be that way. If my will is not free then you cannot blame me if I only do what I am genetically programmed to do. The trouble with such an approach is that it legitimises all kinds of behaviour; from the drunkard claiming it is in his genes, to the rapist saying that he is only doing what he has been programmed to do. On the other hand, if I am free and responsible for what I do, then I cannot be genetically programmed. I do not doubt that there are genetic factors in all aspects of human behaviour but I cannot believe that every human being and their actions are governed by such determinism. A crucial part of being human is having the ability to choose.

Third, your secular morality is not, as you admit, absolute: 'fortunately however morals do not have to be absolute'. As you indicate it is changeable according to the whims of society. Indeed, if we are, as your favourite philosopher Bertrand Russell puts it, 'tiny lumps of impure carbon and water crawling about for a few years, until they are dissolved again into the elements of which they are compounded', there seems to be no basis for absolute morality. You recognise this: 'it is pretty hard to defend absolute morals on grounds other than religious ones'. Why is this important? Because if there are no absolutes then there is no ultimate standard to judge by. And if there is no ultimate standard then we are left with anything goes, might is right, or the whims of a changing and confused society.

And finally, your absolute Darwinian philosophy cannot logically and consistently argue for morality because, to put it bluntly, there is no good or evil. As you so brilliantly describe it in *The Blind Watchmaker:* 'In a universe of blind physical forces and genetic replication, some people are going to get hurt, other people are going to get lucky, and you won't find any rhyme or reason in it, nor any justice. The universe we observe has precisely the properties we should expect if there is at bottom, no design, no purpose, no evil and no good, nothing but blind pitiless indifference.' That then is the atheist basis of morality – no justice, no rhyme nor reason, no purpose, no evil, no good, just blind pitiless indifference. It is little wonder that atheist philosophers have been desperately hunting round to try and establish some basis for a godless morality. Despite the best efforts of atheistic philosophers such as Peter Singer, Princeton Professor of Bioethics and a leading atheist polemicist, this basis is severely lacking, being little more than a utilitarian 'greatest good for the greatest number' without ever defining what 'good' is.

I think you recognise that this is the Achilles heel of atheism and so you go on the attack – ridiculing Christian morality. It has to be admitted that there are many things that have been done in the name of religion, including Christianity, which are inexcusable and that the behaviour of many professing Christians leaves a great deal to be desired. However, you should be careful before denouncing the whole of Christianity on the basis of the behaviour of those who are Christians and fail to be perfect, or of those who, whilst claiming the label Christian, have no more faith than yourself.

Your major case against Christian morality is the Bible itself (we will come on to that in your next chapter) but in this one you throw up a couple of red herrings.

First, at the beginning of the chapter you cite a number of letters which you have received from people you say are Christians. These contain expletives, threats of violence and grotesque language. Why did you cite these at the beginning of a chapter about morality? Because it is again your favourite *ad hominem* tactic. Look how stupid/ignorant/violent/immoral these Christians are and therefore Christian morality is the same. There are two easy counters to that. First, by definition these people cannot be Christians, followers of the one who told his disciples to turn the other cheek, not to threaten violence, not to use foul language and to love our enemies. Second, what would you think if I cited the following from your own website:

XXX David Robertson is a self-righteous narrow minded, up his own XXX thick as pig XXX moronic retard! Watch out David, the sky fairy is late for his second coming and will be angry with you. Why is anyone debateing with this moron? He doesn't know how to! He has the intellectual capacity of road kill.

May your XXX come to life and kiss you. I'm impressed that some of the people here bother to debate this Robertson nincompoop. He is clearly out of his mind and beyond reason and logic. If you do debate him, stop respecting his delusions, however eloquent he puts them, and please approach him with the scorn and contempt that he deserves.

Prat. Bigot. Moron. In fact there are pages and pages of this stuff. It is quite clear that your website acts as a kind of therapy centre for some people but do you think it would be fair for me to say that therefore all atheists are as rude, ignorant and angry?

The second argument you use is to point out that Christian morality cannot be up to much if it requires the threat of hell or some kind of punishment in order to make people behave. You cite Einstein: 'If people are good only because they fear punishment, and hope for reward, then we are a sorry lot indeed.' Einstein is right in at least one thing. We are a sorry lot. Here is a simple test for you. Would you like the police to be removed from Oxford? Do you think that students at your University should be threatened with punishment if they cheat? Or should they be given higher degrees if they do better than their peers? Surely if your students are only studying and not cheating because they fear punishment or have hope for some reward they are a sorry lot? Of course you see the fallacy of the argument. The Bible recognises that human beings are complex and that we need a system of checks and balances to help us – but here is the rub, the Bible's teaching is not primarily moralistic. It is much more radical than that. If it were the carrot and stick approach only, then the Bible would just be recognising the situation for what it is – rather than seeking to change it to a better world.

Let us look then at the Christian case for morality and why, for some people, it is the most important proof for God.

1. It explains evil. The question is not 'why are people good?' but rather 'why are people evil?' Your view of morality seems to stem from your nice middle-class English background. It is a hopelessly optimistic and unfounded view of human nature – that human beings are essentially good and indeed are getting better all the time. Remember the question that I went to University to study – how could a decent civilised nation like the German people allow themselves to get into a position where they eradicated six million Jews plus many homosexuals, gypsies and Christians? It is easy in those circumstances, aided by decades of Hollywood conditioning, to believe that the world is divided into the good guys and the bad guys, and just simply to suggest that the Germans were bad, or Hitler was an insane demon. But my studies led me to the conclusion that the Germans were human and that Hitler was all too human. Indeed, there was an enormous fuss a couple of years ago when the film *Downfall* was shown in Germany because it portrayed Hitler as a human being. The Bible tells us what we would already know if only we opened our eyes, that human beings are screwed up. As Freddy Mercury, late of Queen, sang at the first Live Aid, 'If there's a God up above, a God of love, Then what must he think, of the mess that we've made, of the world that he created?'

2. It explains the universe. Have you ever read C. S. Lewis' 'Right and Wrong as a Clue to the Meaning of the Universe' in his *Mere Christianity*? He, more than anyone, sums up why the moral law is such a powerful proof for the existence of God. He wrote, 'Human beings all over the earth, have

this curious idea that they ought to behave in a certain way, and cannot really get rid of it. Secondly they know that they do not in fact behave in that way. They know the Law of Nature; they break it. These two facts are the foundation of all clear thinking about ourselves and the universe we live in.' Lewis points out that there are two clear evidences for God – the first is the universe he has made. The second is the Moral Law which he argues is a better bit of information because it is 'inside information'. One of the major objections that many people will have to the notion that God created the universe is that things seem so cruel and unjust. But, as Lewis asks, how do we get the idea of cruel and unjust in the first place? What is there in us that makes us aware of right and wrong?

3. It explains me. In looking at the horror of the Holocaust it was the most humbling and awful experience to realise that not only were the Nazis human but I was too. The same evil that came to such horrendous fruition in the Nazis was also, at least in seed form, present in me. Reading books like Gitta Sereny's excellent *Albert Speer; His Battle with Truth*[28] was a sobering experience. As one G. K. Chesterton masterfully put it in a letter to *The Times*: 'Dear Editor: What's wrong with the world? I am. Faithfully yours, G. K. Chesterton.'

But let us return to the atheistic view of morality. I accept fully that you are not a Social Darwinist. You know that that would be wrong. Although I am intrigued as to how you know. But leaving that aside, my fear is that once society as a whole accepts your basic presuppositions (that there are no absolutes in morality, that morality changes and that human nature is genetically determined) then it is a downward slippery slope to

[28] Random House (1995)

the kind of atheistic societies that the world has already seen (such as Stalin's Russia and Mao's China). I am not arguing that all atheists are immoral any more than I am arguing that all professing Christians are moral. All of us live inconsistently with our creeds. However, in Christianity there are brakes, checks and balances and it does not appear immediately obvious that this is the case with atheism. If there is no absolute right or wrong then how can we state that anything is right or wrong?

Take the case of abortion which you discuss in chapter eight. You point out a fascinating fact that 'strong opponents of abortion are almost all deeply religious'. This is a fact that has always puzzled me. Surely any scientist would know that there is nothing that the baby has outside the womb which she does not also have inside the womb. Why then is it considered a human right to be allowed to kill a baby in the womb but not outside it? And there is another question in this debate which fascinates me. In India over 500,000 female fetuses are aborted each year because they are female. Naturally women's groups are objecting to this form of selective abortion. But why? Why would pro-abortionists want to interfere with a woman's right to choose not to have a girl? Is it not after all the woman's body? Besides which, in the eyes of pro-abortionists, it's not a girl but a 'potential' girl. The inconsistencies are ironic.

Of course, once we move away from the simplistic and unscientific 'a woman has a right to choose to kill the baby in her womb but not outside of it', then we can end up with all kinds of difficulties. Peter Singer argues that 'mentally impaired babies have no greater rights than certain animals'.[29]

Bill Hamilton, to whom you owed a great deal in the writing of your book *The Selfish Gene* – and whose writing you stated was passionate, vivid and informed – was an excellent Darwinian biologist whose views were certainly of a different

[29] *Independent Extra* (13 September 2006)

kind of morality. He once said that he had more sympathy for a lone fern than he did for a crying child. He argued that males were largely doomed to compete and that the purpose of sex was to clean out the gene pool by filtering out the useless and the weak. The low status male would be better off dead. Everything in nature according to Hamilton could be explained as the outcome of competition between genes. He argued for a radical programme of infanticide, eugenics and euthanasia in order to save the world. He believed that modern medicine was doing harm by allowing the weak to survive and thus preserving their genes. His two concrete examples of these are caesarean sections and the glasses worn by John Maynard Smith! Spectacles were a symbol of decadence within the gene pool and as for caesarean sections – women should be allowed one and then only to save the mother's life – after that they should be paid not to have any more children.

Hamilton's view of modern medicine was so eugenically based that he believed that the only acceptable forms of medicine were painkillers and surgery. He declared that genocide was the result of over-breeding and that he would grieve more for the death of one giant panda than he would for a 'hundred unknown Chinese'. He also argued that the handicapped should be killed at birth. In arguing for what he termed 'inclusive happiness' he stated, 'I have little doubt that if trying to survive on Robinson Crusoe's island with my wife I would indeed with my own hands kill a defective baby.' In this, he and Singer would be as one.

It may be that the extreme social and political views of Hamilton are in fact an exception and that it would not be right to tar all biologists with the same brush. That is true. It is not biologists who are the problem but some biologists who also happen to be atheists and who do not accept the notion of an absolute morality. And whilst Hamilton may have been on the extreme there have been plenty others who have worked out the logical conclusion to their atheistic materialism. Some of the leading evolutionary biologists in the 20th century have been people who, because of their atheistic philosophy and misunderstanding of science, adopted extreme political views. Konrad Lorenz was an enthusiastic Nazi. J. B. S. Haldane was a committed Stalinist and R. A. Fisher used to argue that civilisation was threatened because upper class women (i.e. 'quality') did not have enough babies.

At this point, perhaps, someone might point out that I am doing the same thing to you that I accuse you of doing to others – namely picking some extremes and using them to condemn the lot. The difference is this. Whereas you cite people who are on the wacky fringes of Christianity the people I am speaking about are key and central figures. Can you imagine how atheists would have reacted if the Archbishop of Canterbury, the Pope or Billy Graham had come out arguing for infanticide, banning caesarean sections, or encouraging the 'superior' classes to breed more than the common people?! We would never have heard the end of it.

Meanwhile, you cite such fringe characters as Fred Phelps of Westboro Baptist Church and ignore the substantial history and philosophy within the grounds of atheistic secular biology of those who have advocated such extreme social views. What was most disturbing about Nazism was not whether its main thinkers were 'nice' people, but rather its philosophical foundation and the basis and justification it gave for cruelty and injustice. That is the same for Social Darwinism where the elimination of the weak and the destruction of the handicapped are the very antithesis of Christianity and the real enemy of humanity. I repeat again, for the umpteenth time, that this is not to state that all evolutionary atheists are *de facto* fascists, but it is to say that the logical consequences of evolutionary atheism can easily lead, and has led, to such a position.

The Christian view of morality is not, as most people suppose, that the Bible gives us a set of laws to live by. Real Christians are not moralists – thinking that if only we offer a reward here, a bit of punishment there, then 'decent' human beings will behave better and somehow earn their own stairway to heaven. We know that we can neither legislate nor use religion to make us good. Real Christians realise that the Bible's teaching is that there is an absolute morality – from which we all fall short. And no amount of religion, good works or pious acts will ever be able to make us right. That is where grace, salvation, the cross and all the wonderful truths of the acts of God in Christ come into their own. God was in Christ reconciling the world to himself. That is why the Gospel is Good News. Not because it gives us a set of laws to live by, or religious rites to perform, but because it deals with the biggest problem in the world – the problem of the human heart. It is for that reason that every year I religiously watch *Schindler's List* to remind me of why I am a minister of the Christian Gospel. I don't just want to explain the Darkness. I want to defeat it.

Yours, etc.

David

LETTER 9 –
THE MYTH OF THE IMMORAL BIBLE

Dear Dr Dawkins,

In chapter three you had a go at the Bible but now you really stick the boot in. The belief in the Bible as instruction or moral example 'encourages a system of morals which any civilised modern person, whether religious or not, would find – I can put it no more gently – obnoxious.... Those who wish to base their morality literally on the Bible have either not read it or not understood it, as Bishop John Shelby Spong, in *The Sins of Scripture*, rightly observed.'

I have studied the Bible for over 25 years. For 20 of those it has been my job to do so. I have tried to do so with an open mind and a desire to know what it really says. At times it has puzzled me, caused me to question and has presented me with seemingly insurmountable difficulties. I hope that you would grant me as a professional in this field of study, the same respect I grant you as a biologist. Your understanding of Scripture is extreme in its condemnation and seems governed more by your atheism than by any knowledge or understanding of the text. Yet you prejudge the whole issue at the beginning of this chapter by again implying that those who do not accept your point of view are not civilised, moral or intelligent enough to understand the Bible. This is yet again another one of those 'Emperor has no clothes' moments. You imply that only those who see the Bible as immoral are intelligent and moral. There is almost nothing I can say to people with such presuppositions but let me at least try to help those who are inclined to accept at face value your distorted and sour-grape-picking version of the Bible.

In your attack on the Bible you mention Noah's Ark, Sodom and Gomorrah, The Levite concubines in Judges, Abraham lying, the almost sacrifice of Isaac, Jephthah's daughter, the Golden Calf, Moses attacking the Midianites, all in the Old Testament (and for good measure you throw in Pat Robertson and New Orleans, although quite what that has to do with the Bible escapes me). In the New Testament your objections seem to be that Jesus was rude to his mother and had dodgy family values, and the doctrine of the atonement. In addition to this you try to dismiss the positive teachings in the Bible of 'do not kill' and 'love your neighbour' as actually racist, meaning 'do not kill Jews' and 'love only fellow Jews'. You go so far as to state that, 'Jesus would have turned over in his grave if he had known that Paul would be taking his plan to the pigs.' It's all wonderful knock about stuff for your fans, equivalent to the kind of comedy that George Carlin, whom you cite, is famous for. But, it is a long way from what the Bible actually says.

First, anyone who reads the Bible in its context cannot take seriously the suggestion that Jesus only came for the Jews and that 'love your neighbour' only meant the Jews. The very parable that Jesus told to illustrate that truth was one which involved a non-Jew. Your re-writing and re-reading of these verses is out of context, dishonest and deceitful special pleading which says a whole lot more about your prejudgements than it does about the Bible. You base much of your thinking here on what you call a 'remarkable paper' by John Hartung, an associate professor of anaesthesiology and an anthropologist. This paper, entitled 'Love Thy Neighbor: The Evolution of In-Group Morality', includes an acknowledgement of you and your wife and more disturbingly a sympathetic review of Kevin MacDonald's *A People that Shall Dwell Alone: Judaism as a Group Evolutionary Strategy*.[30] It is all getting disturbingly close to the 'evolutionary' view of religion and Judaism that the Nazi academics and scientists taught. And it is a million miles away from what the Bible actually says.

Second, Pat Robertson, New Orleans, and the various twisted theologies of some exponents of Christianity have nothing to do with the teachings of the Scriptures, which should be judged on their own merits.

Third, you need to learn the basic principles of reading the Bible. You must always read it in context – that includes historical, literary, theological and biblical context. To read out of context is to misread. Then you must recognise that much of the Bible is descriptive rather than prescriptive. In other words, it is telling us what went on rather than what should have happened. In fact, this is one of the things that helped convince me of the truth of the Bible. Most of the main characters, even the heroes, come out quite badly. They are painted warts and all. If this was myth why would someone write about such things as David committing murder and adultery, or Abraham lying about his wife?

Atheists are fond of arguing against what they consider to be 'literal' interpretations of the Bible. Like some fundamentalists you consider those who are not literalists as just cowards. But it really does depend on what you mean by 'literal'. When I am asked if I read the Bible literally I can never answer directly because I need to know first of all what the questioner means. If he means do I take every word at its literal meaning then the answer is no, of course not. When Jesus said 'I am the vine', he did not mean that he was green and produced literal grapes. To read any literature in such a way, never mind such an extensive collection of books as the Bible, would be plain stupid and false

[30] Greenwood Press (1994)

to the book itself. The Bible has at least five different genres: prophecy, poetry, history, letter and law. On the other hand, if by literal you mean 'at face value' then yes, I do read the Bible literally. You ask 'by what criteria do you decide which passages are symbolic, which literal?' The answer – context, genre and common sense. I really do not expect to be dressed in white and playing a harp in heaven (aka the Book of Revelation) but I have no doubt that Jesus literally rose from the dead. It was not symbolic of anything, it was written not as poetry but as verifiable history, and it is a fact that is repeated several times. It is quite clear what the Bible means when it speaks about the resurrection. Mind you, if you seriously believe that when Jesus taught the Old Testament refrain 'love your neighbour', he meant only Jews, then I guess you can make the Bible say whatever you do or do not want it to say!

One important principle is that of progressive revelation. This is the idea that the Bible, written over a period of more than 1000 years, progressively reveals God to us. Little by little the curtain is opened and the light comes in. Therefore, some aspects of earlier revelation are superseded by the later.

Another significant principle is one that you state yourself when trying to defend the horrific statements of such enlightened and liberal atheists as H. G. Wells and Thomas Huxley. The latter declared, 'No rational man, cognizant of the facts, believes that the average negro is the equal, still less the superior, of the white man.' Yet, in order to defend them, you declare, 'It is a commonplace that good historians don't judge statements from past times by the standards of their own.' Exactly. Please apply that to the Bible as well.

I believe the Bible is the Word of God; as such it is true, without error and communicates all that God wants it to. That does not mean it is without problems but I would like to suggest that if you read it bearing in mind the basic principles above, then 90% of the problems you cite will disappear. However that leaves the other 10%. It would be foolish to deny that there are major difficulties within the Bible. There are parts of it that make me feel distinctly uncomfortable and that I struggle with. But who am I to sit in judgement upon the Bible?

Not long after becoming a Christian there were parts in the Bible that greatly disturbed me. I read a book that purported to deal with most of those difficulties; however it did not really help much. But I made a decision that it was stupid and arrogant of me as a young Christian to think that I alone could understand the Bible, and to attempt to sit in judgement upon it. It was not that it was wrong to question but rather that I had to be patient, humble and thoughtful. After more than 25 years studying it I have come more and more to appreciate the truth, wisdom, beauty and relevance of the Bible. This is not because I have to, or I am paid to – in many ways it would have been so much easier to give in and go with the flow; it would certainly have made for an easier life. But I could not, in all intellectual honesty, give up. As a result, I have found the Bible to be more reliable and relevant than anything. I find it amazing, when I teach even parts that seem more obscure and difficult, that it addresses the needs, desires and lives of ordinary people living in the 21st century. I would venture a guess that many of the 'atheist' converts from religion are those who have never really drunk deep from the well of Scripture. For me, to paraphrase the words of B. B. King, 'the thrill has not gone'.

You clearly have difficulty with the atonement as well. 'I have described atonement, the central doctrine of Christianity, as vicious, sadomasochistic and repellent. We should also dismiss it as barking mad, but for its ubiquitous familiarity which has dulled our objectivity. If God wanted to forgive our sins, why not just forgive them?' Whilst I am grateful that you at least recognise, unlike some professing Christians, that the atonement is the central doctrine of Christianity, it is sad that you are obviously missing out on the best part of the whole Bible. The cross has always been a stumbling block both for the religious and those who consider themselves to be wise. Polly Toynbee, a *Guardian* columnist, was scathing about this when she reviewed *The Lion, the Witch and the Wardrobe*.[31] She vehemently declared that she did not need anyone to die for her sins.

For most people, the notion that we have done anything so bad as to deserve death *is* repellent. But that is because we do not have an adequate understanding of evil and sin. And we have no real awareness of the depths of depravity in our own hearts. Once you grasp that then the doctrine of atonement – the idea that the Son of God died in my place and paid the price for my sin – is a truth that is wonderful. It's the best part of the whole Bible. What would be repellent would be if Rousseau's reputed last words were true; he claimed that God would forgive him because 'c'est son metier' (that's his job). So, no matter what we do or how we behave God will forgive us. Such cheap forgiveness is neither just nor biblical.

The most interesting and disturbing part of this chapter is the section headed 'The Moral Zeitgeist', which examines the changing moral cultures. Here you are expounding a fairly common belief that atheists hold – that things are getting better all the time. Humanity is evolving from a primitive morality to a generally improved moral consensus. This of course is highly questionable and the evidence you offer for such chronological (and indeed Western) snobbery is scanty. Is it really the case that the moral *zeitgeist* is improving in Britain and the US? Are women really being treated better? Has racism and prejudice been done away with? Is our current sex-obsessed, materialistic and shallow society better than it was one hundred years ago?

[31] 'Narnia represents everything that is most hateful about religion', Polly Toynbee, The *Guardian* (5 December 2005)

That is not immediately self-evident! Of course there have been vast improvements but sometimes one wonders whether it is one step forward and two steps back. I suspect that only a nice middle-class Western moralist could be so confident and glib about the greatly improving moral situation with humanity. I had thought that such liberal utopianism had received a mortal blow after the First World War and was killed off after the Second. But apparently not. You are once again teaching that the human race is evolving to moral perfection and that the only thing that is preventing us from realising this is the evil of religion.

You cite as examples of the improved moral *zeitgeist* increased female suffrage and a change in attitude to race. You mention that even Washington, Jefferson and other 'men of the Enlightenment' held slaves (curious that you are prepared to excuse this practice in these men because it was 250 years ago but you condemn it in the Old Testament 2000 years ago). Most shocking of all you point out that H. G. Wells in his *New Republic* in answering the question as to how the New Republic would deal with the 'inferior races' such as the black, the yellow man, etc. stated, 'Well, the world is a world, and not a charitable institution, and I take it they will have to go.' He made it quite clear what he meant – the extermination of inferior races. You state that this position would now be unacceptable in society and more astonishingly you claim that this is because of 'improved education and in particular, the increased understanding that each of us shares a common humanity with members of other races and with the other sex – both deeply unbiblical ideas that come from biological science, especially evolution.' When I read that I had to stop and take a deep breath. Did he really write that? Does he really have the audacity to think that he can get away with such a big lie?!

The Bible taught a long time ago (Genesis 1) that both men and women were made in the image of God. The Bible also taught that all human beings, of whatever race, were descendants of Adam and that all were made in the image of God. To describe these ideas as unbiblical when they are foundational to the Bible is bad enough. But then to suggest that it is evolution which has led us away from the evils of Wells *et al.* is breathtaking. The Church was teaching long before the end of the 19th century that all human beings were made in the image of God. Last year I visited a Black University in South Africa where one of the photos on the wall was of a Black South African who had come to study in Glasgow and returned as an ordained Presbyterian minister in the 19th century. It was not the Church nor the Bible that was teaching that 'inferior races' should be destroyed. In fact, you cite Huxley's racism (*Emancipation – Black and White* – published in 1865) as typical of the *zeitgeist* of the time. Yet Huxley was arguing against the *zeitgeist*. Society, led primarily by Christian activists and thinkers working on biblical principles, had come to the conclusion that slavery was wrong. William Wilberforce, the British parliamentarian, made his first abolition motion in 1789. Motivated by his Christian biblical understanding that all human beings were created in the image of God, he presented no fewer than 11 abolition bills to the House of Commons until finally, in 1807, the slave trade was abolished. After further campaigning slavery itself was abolished in 1833. Britain then sought to persuade other slaving nations to reject slavery – the government bought Portuguese and Spanish abolition for over £1 million and French in exchange for military aid. The British navy enforced this abolition over a period of 50 years spending £40 million seizing 1,600 ships to liberate 150,000 slaves.

Twenty years before Huxley, in the 1840s, my own church, St Peters in Dundee, was holding anti-slavery meetings and acting as a focus for supporting the anti-slavery movement in the US. And yet Huxley was arguing that this biblical morality was unscientific. He believed what he believed not because of the *zeitgeist* but because of his science. It was such Social

Darwinian evolutionary thinking that fed the manic utopianism of Wells and others. I am grateful that the *zeitgeist* of atheistic evolutionary biologists has improved more recently but please do not put us all in the same boat.

Which brings me on nicely to the six pages you devote to Stalin and Hitler. I can understand why atheists want to dissociate themselves from the like of Stalin, Mao and Pol Pot – after all they were the leaders of the only officially atheistic states so far, and their human-rights record was, shall we say, not exactly great. The only argument I have heard atheists use is that, well, really, Stalin was not an atheist because he behaved unreasonably and unreasonable people cannot be atheists! It's the ultimate in circular arguments and there is no point in trying to break into the circle.

However Hitler is different. You want to cite Hitler as a Christian, although even you know that is going a bit far. As already indicated this is one subject that I have studied extensively. The basic facts are as follows: Hitler was brought up as a Catholic; when he came to power he did so in a situation where the Catholic Church and the Lutheran Church were still significant social forces within German society; he was quite happy to use the Christian churches and Christian symbols when he could; ironically it was those who taught as you do – that religion should be privatised and that the Church should stay out of politics – who provided the biggest reason for non-opposition to Hitler. Thankfully men like Dietrich Bonhoeffer and others were prepared to ignore that advice and do what they could to resist evil. Bonhoeffer even put into print an accusation that Hitler was anti-Christian, and attacked the 'Blood and Soil' ideology of the Nazis ('He may call this ideology Christian, but in doing so he becomes Christ's enemy.'[32]) For this bravery, based again upon his Christian faith, he paid the ultimate sacrifice.

[32] Bonhoeffer *Discipleship*.

If we really want to know what Hitler thought, his actions and above all his private words are the most compelling evidence. And I am grateful to you for citing Hitler's *Table Talk*, which tells us conclusively what Hitler thought about Christianity: 'The heaviest blow that ever struck humanity was the coming of Christianity.' Even more interesting is the following from Traudl Junge, Hitler's personal secretary:

Sometimes we also had interesting discussions about the church and the development of the human race. Perhaps it's going too far to call them discussions, because he would begin explaining his ideas when some question or remark from one of us had set them off, and we just listened. He was not a member of any church, and thought the Christian religions were outdated, hypocritical institutions that lured people into them. The laws of nature were his religion. He could reconcile his dogma of violence better with nature than with the Christian doctrine of loving your neighbour and your enemy. 'Science isn't yet clear about the origins of humanity,' he once said. 'We are probably the highest stage of development of some mammal which developed from reptiles and moved on to human beings, perhaps by way of the apes. We are a part of creation and children of nature, and the same laws apply to us as to all living creatures. And in nature the law of the struggle for survival has reigned from the first. Everything incapable of life, everything weak is eliminated. Only mankind and above all the church have made it their aim to keep alive the weak, those unfit to live, and people of an inferior kind.[33]

That just about says it all.

You ask at the end of this chapter, 'Why would someone go to war for the sake of an absence of belief?' I assume by that you

[33] *Until the Final Hour* p. 108

mean an absence of belief in God. The answer to your question is twofold. First, it could be that the reason people go to war *is* the absence of belief. If, like Stalin or Hitler, you believe that there is no God to answer to, that 'might is right' and that power comes at the end of a gun, then you are much more likely to indulge your selfish genes and go to war to get what you want. The second answer to your question is in the quote above. Hitler clearly did not go to war because he believed in God or because he wanted to spread Christianity. He hated Christianity. On the other hand he did believe that religion was a virus (where have I heard that one before?) and that the Jews especially were vermin who should be eradicated in order better to preserve the species. It was all perfectly logical, Darwinian and godless. Perhaps the atheist *zeitgeist* has moved on. But meanwhile, until it is proven otherwise, I would prefer to stick with the tried and tested morality of the Bible.

Yours, etc.
David

LETTER 10 –
THE MYTH OF RELIGIOUS CHILD ABUSE

Dear Dr Dawkins,

You ask, 'Isn't it also a form of child abuse to label children as possessors of beliefs that they are too young to have thought about?' This question is the whole purpose of your chapter nine. Your view that children should not be taught religion you illustrate with a horror story of the kidnapping of an Italian Jewish boy in the 19th century; abuse by the Catholic Church; an interview with Pastor Keenan Roberts who sets up Hell Houses to educate children; testimonies from people brought up in Christian homes who are now atheists; a wee go at the Amish; a six-page attack on Emmanuel school in the North East of England and an appeal against the labelling of children on the basis of their parents' religion. You finish by arguing that religious education should be about learning the Bible as literature. All in all, those who are atheists will share your horror at what you call this religious child abuse and others may be influenced to think that perhaps you will have a case. But let me suggest that there are yet again major flaws in your argument.

You underplay the role of sexual abuse in order to demonstrate the horrors of the psychological abuse caused to children. You openly admit that you were a victim of child sexual abuse in your English boarding school from a teacher 'whose affection for small boys overstepped the bounds of propriety'; something you describe as 'an embarrassing but otherwise harmless experience'. This leads you to talk about the horrific child abuse cases that have come to light regarding the Catholic church, and then to make the extraordinary statement that 'horrible as sexual abuse no doubt was, the damage was arguably less than the long-term psychological damage inflicted by bringing up the child Catholic in the first place' (a comment which you inform us was made to an audience of Dublin intellectuals and received spontaneous applause). And it is not just the Catholics you have a go at – although you do seem to have a particular disdain for both them and American evangelicals. You also mention the Exclusive Brethren, a 'more than unusually odious sect'. Later on you come to the Amish and in a few disparaging sentences suggest that modern society is guilty of allowing Amish parents to abuse their children.

All this is of course leading to an inevitable and shocking conclusion. If the situation is as you say and religion is a virus then the logical thing is to protect children. You cite with evident approval the psychologist Nicholas Humphrey:

> Children, I'll argue, have a human right not to have their minds crippled by exposure to other people's bad ideas – no matter who those other people are.... So we should no more allow parents to teach their children to believe, for example, in the literal truth of the Bible or that the planets rule their lives, than we should allow parents to knock their children's teeth out or to lock them in a dungeon.

We are almost coming full circle here. You began with the story about the kidnapping of Edgardo Mortara, who was taken away from his parents because a servant had baptised him as a Catholic and his parents were Jewish. The Catholic authorities were prepared to 'save' the boy from the Jewish upbringing that they believed would cause him harm. You are rightly horrified by this and yet you have now moved on to an almost similar position.

I have taught and will continue to teach my children that the Bible is true and you are now accusing me of doing them more harm than if I sexually abused them. Perhaps in the Brave New World of the Atheist State the religious thought police will be sent round to ensure that my children are being taught 'correct' thoughts. If it is right for the State to take children away from parents who would sexually abuse them, and if you believe that bringing a child up in the Christian faith is more abusive, then logically you must believe that the State should have the right to remove children from such abusive situations. If you follow your logic through then the story of Edgardo Mortara will be the story of many more children, whose parents do not accept the atheist *zeitgeist* of the new moral order. As Marilynn Robinson, the brilliant and perceptive author of the best novel of the past century, *Gilead*, points out:

> And how might it have been worse? If the child had fallen, as in the next century so many would, into the hands of those who considered his Jewishness biological rather than religious and cultural. To Dawkins's objection that Nazi science was not authentic science I would reply, first, that neither Nazis nor Germans had any monopoly on these theories, which were influential throughout the Western world, and second, that the research on human subjects carried out by those holding such assumptions was good enough science to appear in medical texts for fully half a century. This is not to single out science as exceptionally inclined to do harm, though its capacity for doing harm is by now unequalled. It is only to note that science, too, is implicated in this bleak human proclivity, and is one major instrument of it.[34]

[34] Review of *The God Delusion* in *Harper's Magazine*, November 2006, reproduced online at http://darwiniana.com/2006/10/23/marilynne-robinson-on-dawkins/

The notion that keeping children away from religion will somehow save the world is a fanciful one which ignores logic, common sense and human history. As regards the latter, I am reminded of an asylum seeker in the Netherlands whom I met last year. She is an educated doctor from Azerbaijan. She has experienced the horrors of religious ethnic cleansing – having been forced from her country by Muslim fundamentalists. You would expect that having experienced the evil effects of some religion she would have been supportive of your point of view. But when I discussed it with her she completely disagreed with you. 'We spent 70 years,' she told me, '70 years when we were not allowed to be taught about God. We lived in an atheist state where only atheism was taught. They even tried to ban God from our homes.' The results were all too clearly seen in the atheist Soviet Union. The philosophy and ideas you put forward in this chapter have been tried already and, as already pointed out, they have been a spectacular failure.

It does scare me a little that the basic position you outline in this chapter is one which labels me both as abused and abuser. I was brought up in the Brethren. There are aspects of it I did not like and I met some strange people and heard some strange things. However, I also met some wonderful people and was taught some wonderful things – not least that I should use my own mind. It was doing precisely that which caused me first of all to reject the faith I had been brought up with and secondly to return, not to Brethrenism, but to Jesus Christ. My childhood was largely a happy one within the context of a loving family and an open community. Yet you think I would have been better off being sexually abused by some boarding school master than being brought up having been taught about Jesus Christ. And you accuse me of being worse than a paedophile because I happily teach young children that God loves them, that they are important and have a purpose and a place in his world. Is it little wonder that people think that your logic is a bit twisted by your secular fundamentalism and are they not right to be more than a little frightened by the consequences of such a perverse view?

Speaking of schools your American readers must be wondering why you spend six pages attacking one state school in the North East of England. What kind of evil and horrendous place is this that it results in you, the Bishop of Oxford and almost all the English intelligentsia uniting to condemn and attack it? Emmanuel College is a state school. In Britain we do not have a formal separation of Church and State and therefore many state schools are meant to be based upon a Christian ethos. A considerable number of schools in England are Anglican and it is still the case that most schools have at least one act of public Christian worship per week. However, much of the state system in Britain is in crisis – the fact that the decline in standards has arisen at the same time as the decline in Christianity and the rise of secularism may or may not be apposite. Many of the poorest are being left behind in run-down schools with very poor academic records. The government, for better or for worse, has tried to encourage rich benefactors to invest in State schools in poorer areas known as 'city academies'.

One person who has invested is Sir Peter Vardy, a millionaire businessman and a Christian. One of the three schools he has supported, to the tune of £2 million each, is Emmanuel College, Gateshead, in the North East of England. So why are you, and so many of your friends, so bitterly opposed to this school? Why in a book about 'the God Delusion', and a chapter about religious child abuse, do you devote so much space to attacking this school and calling it an educational scandal? Because the head of science, Stephen Layfield, is a Christian and wrote a paper on the 'The teaching of science: a biblical perspective'. In this he commits the cardinal sin of daring to question evolution.

Now he may or may not be wrong – and I am sure that if the basic principles of science are taught then his pupils will soon be able to discern the truth. But are you really justified in labelling Emmanuel Christian School as a place where child abuse is taking place? Are you right to label it a 'creationist college' which brainwashes students to accept the biblical view uncritically?

I decided to find out and not surprisingly the truth is somewhat different. The policy of the College is to teach the arguments for and against evolution, intelligent design, etc. Students are encouraged to take a critical approach and not to accept things without subjecting them to scrutiny and discussion. Teachers and students are encouraged to state their own views. Of the nine science staff three would hold to a young-earth creationist position, three to a theistic evolutionist position and three are non-Christian evolutionists. Does this sound like a school that is designed to ignore current scientific thinking? As far as I can recall it reflects my own experience of school where my chemistry teacher was an atheist, my physics teacher was a Christian and my biology teacher was a young-earth creationist. They were all good teachers who did not seek to impose their views. So why are you so bitterly opposed to Emmanuel?

This is made even more puzzling when we look at how well Emmanuel is doing. In March 2006 Emmanuel received its third 'outstanding' rating from Ofsted – one of only twelve schools in the country at the time. August saw exam results that placed the College in the top five comprehensive schools in England. This is not a school in the elitist green suburbs of Oxford. It is a school in one of the poorest areas of England and its 1250 pupils are receiving an excellent education in a good school. Surely, as a liberal humanitarian you should be delighting in this success – even if the head of science has views which you consider to be wrong. Your attitude to this is puzzling and smacks more of the fundamentalist ethos than a liberal humanitarian view which sees education as a good in and of itself.

It is worth noticing that the campaign against this highly successful school was begun by the National Secular Society. Why? Why have they not begun a campaign to raise all our schools to the level and standards of Emmanuel? Why are they not shouting from the rooftops at the scandal of the declining education system in our country, especially for the poor, instead of attacking a school that is actually working? It is because they are more concerned for their ideology than they are for people. I even know one official of that society who, whilst publicly campaigning against any sort of Christian influence in state schools, sends his own children to a private Christian school because 'they get a better education there'. Hypocrisy.

Speaking of hypocrisy you mention Dan Barker, a former fundamentalist minister who continued to preach for a while even after he became an atheist, who says that he knows 'many other American clergymen who are in the same position as he was but have confided only in him, having read his book'. I do not dispute this. There are many theoretical Christians who are in reality practising atheists in the Church. This is especially true when religion can be seen as a way to make money or make a living. If someone no longer believes then of course they should not continue to take a salary from an organisation they no longer support, teaching doctrines they no longer believe in.

Coming from a working-class background I did not go to boarding schools and I do not have the money to buy my children the 'best' education. I am more than happy to send them to state schools but I do not want them to be indoctrinated by the minority of secularists and atheists who seem to think that their philosophy is the only one which should have any credence. I have noticed that although atheists talk the talk about education, when it comes to walking the walk, they do not generally build schools or put their money where their mouth is. Instead they prefer to seize, cuckoo-like, the work, money and initiatives of others so that they can then use these to teach on the basis of their own philosophy.

My own country, Scotland, was famous for its education system, a system that provided opportunity, education and advancement for all who were prepared to take it. It was a system that was based upon Christian principles and operated on the notion of where there was a church there should be a school. All our major Universities were founded on Christian principles and in general that system has served us well. It is no coincidence that as the basic principles of Christianity have been driven out of school and culture Scotland has become a significantly dumbed down culture and we are rapidly slipping down the international educational league table.

I do not want a Stalinist system which bans Christianity from school and home. Nor do I want an American secularist model that leaves the wealthy and middle class to send their children to private schools (often based on Christian principles) whilst often allowing the poor to rot in an under-funded state system based on a poor philosophy of education. Teaching children on the basis of Christian principles of love, mutual respect, inquiry, truth and justice is not abuse. Denying children the opportunity to a decent education because of the bias of your philosophy – that is abuse. And accusing parents who seek to bring their children up in the love and peace of Christ of being child abusers is contemptible.

There is however one area where I can agree with you. You lament the biblical illiteracy of our current society. I agree. Totally. Mind you, it is only such ignorance which means that you can get away with many of the claims you make about the Bible in your books. Anyone who is biblically literate would soon recognise that your representation of the Bible is distorted and out of context. What may shock you even more (it certainly depresses me) is how biblically illiterate many professing Christians are. If Christians knew the Word better and were better taught, we would not have much to fear from the resurgent atheism you are trying to encourage. The Bible is so much more than an interesting literary and cultural collection. It is the living and enduring Word of God. Heaven and earth will pass away but the Word of God will endure forever.

Let's move briefly on to chapter ten. This is a somewhat strange and disjointed chapter which skirts over the notion of religion as some kind of consolation, the Christian attitude to death and ends up with the theories of quantum physics. You seem to think that those of us who believe in God are in effect children who have not grown out of the need for an imaginary friend. Apart from the patronising aspect of this, the question arises to me that if the God of the Bible, or the God of the Catholics or the God of anyone is as horrible as you state, how can belief in him be a consolation?

As regards death, you imply that if we really believed what we said then we would all be happy about dying. Of course, if we all went delirious to the grave you would then be citing this as evidence of the power of religion to brainwash! One of the reasons I believe is precisely because of death. It would be so easy and such a relief in some ways to believe that once I died that was it. Imagine no afterlife. No one to answer to. No heaven. No hell. Nothing unknown. Just death, stillness and nothingness. To believe that would for many people be bliss. It is little wonder that some of your converts describe such a belief with religious fervour. And yet I have tried that route. And it just does not work. It does not work because it does not ring true. It does not work because there is something inside me that tells me there is more to life than this life. It does not work because the whole universe screams out the majesty and glory of God. It does not work because I have a mind which tells me that I am neither an inanimate object nor just a collection of molecules on their way to nothing. It does not work because I know that my body is more than a throwaway survival machine, just as I know that the world is not flat and life is not meaningless. The atheist answer to death is found in Camus' *L'Etranger* (*The Stranger*). It is hopeless. The Christian answer is vastly different. It is Christ.

In reviewing your book I think we have come across two competing philosophies. They actually don't have all that much to do with science except insofar as both will cite the discoveries of science as evidence. Your philosophy of logical positivism means that your science replaces God. It is your worldview. It is your life. It is your faith. No wonder that you are so religious in defending it and so keen on rooting out heretics and wishy-washy appeasers! In chapter ten you talk about 'removing the Burka' meaning removing the limited view we have of Middle World (I think Tolkien should sue!). You suggest that now we see only partially but soon science will enable us to see clearly. I was blind but now I see. It's almost Messianic in its fervour and biblical in its language: 'For now we see through a glass, darkly; but then face to face' (1 Corinthians 13:12, KJV).

And this last chapter is where you finally and completely blow away any pretension that your view is based upon empirical, observable, testable evidence. Throughout the book you have been using the existence of the material as the lens through which we are to judge everything. You flavour this with what you deem to be commonsense experience and especially probability. And yet in chapter ten you move way beyond that. You cite Steve Grand, a computer scientist who specialises in artificial intelligence: 'Matter flows from place to place and momentarily comes together to be you. Whatever you are, therefore, you are not the stuff of which you are made. If that doesn't make the hair stand up on the back of your neck, read it again until it does, because it is important.' Grand also goes on to argue that if you remember an experience from your childhood you should remember that you were not really there. 'What we see of the real world is not the unvarnished real world but a model of the real world, regulated and adjusted by sense data – a model that is constructed so that it is useful for dealing with the real world.' This is brilliant stuff which seems to fit with the spiritual, and perhaps even with the biblical notion of the soul, but it is a million miles away from the empirical evidence that you keep demanding. In fact most of it is highly entertaining guesswork – trying to explain and fill in the gaps that science cannot answer. I call it ABGism – Anything-But-God-ism.

Your final sentence declares, 'Even better, we may eventually discover that there are no limits.' Of course you don't mean that. Because you draw the line at God. You cannot believe in a God who created the universe (that's a limit). You refuse to believe in a God who raised Jesus from the dead (another limit). And you ridicule the notion that this God could communicate with human beings through his Spirit and his Word (another limit). You are only prepared to accept no limits in terms of human knowledge. Indeed you want to replace God with humanity. You want us as the Higher Consciousness, to become like God. I believe that a long time ago there was someone else who once offered humanity the key to all knowledge. We fell for it then and have ever since been paying the price. I pray that we will not fall for that one again.

Yours, etc.
David

FINAL LETTER TO THE READER – WHY BELIEVE?

Dear Reader,

Thanks for reading this far (or if you are the kind of person who starts a book backwards – thanks for beginning here!). I promised that I would provide a reading list and some other resources and so space permitting I will do so. I also want to answer a question that has continually been asked me over the past few weeks and one I promised I would answer. But let's do the books first.

I have read over 100 books and articles relating to the subjects covered in these letters. It has been an exhausting but stimulating journey. Some material has stretched my mind until it hurt – especially the quantum physics! I take comfort in the fact that as Richard Feynman pointed out, 'if you think you understand quantum theory … you don't understand quantum theory'. Perhaps the most helpful books have been the following. (Please note that 'helpful' does not necessarily mean an endorsement of everything in every book. I am assuming that those of you who have managed to read this far are grown up enough to realise that we can sometimes learn a lot from people we disagree with. The books below are books I have interacted with – there is only one book I would regard to be absolutely trustworthy, the Bible!).

Obviously *The God Delusion*[35] is the book I am interacting with. If you already have the book then you will know what I am referring to. If you don't, I cannot honestly recommend that you should get it. It really is as bad as I have tried to demonstrate and I would be reluctant to put any more money into it! If you are interested in science then Dawkins' other books are much more palatable. In terms of the science/religion interaction I would recommend:

Alister McGrath, *Dawkins' God: Genes, Memes and the Meaning of Life*;[36] *The Twilight of Atheism*[37] and *Science and Religion: An Introduction*.[38] (I have not yet read *The Dawkins Delusion?*[39] by Alister McGrath and Joanna Collicutt McGrath as, at the time of writing it had not been published; however, I have little doubt that it will be up to McGrath's usual excellent standard.) Kirsten Birkett *Unnatural Enemies: An Introduction to Science and Christianity*[40] is a beautiful little primer on the whole subject and her *The Essence of Psychology*[41] is equally worthwhile. Stephen J. Gould's *Rocks of Ages: Science and Religion in the Fullness of Life*[42] is a mine of information as well. Malcolm A. Jeeves and R. J. Berry, *Science, Life and Christian Belief*[43] has been very helpful to me. For those interested in the history of science and religion David N. Livingstone, *Darwin's Forgotten Defenders: The Encounter Between Evangelical Theology and Evolutionary Thought*[44] is fascinating. For a 19th-century populist writer who is as good as Dawkins in communicating

[35] Hardback: Bantam Press (2006); Paperback: Black Swan (2007)
[36] Blackwell Publishing (2004)
[37] Rider & Co (2004)
[38] Blackwell Publishers (1998)
[39] SPCK Publishing (2007)
[40] Matthias Press (1997)
[41] Matthias Press (1999)
[42] Ballantine Books (1999)
[43] Apollos (1998)
[44] Eerdmans (1987)

his message, but has the distinct advantage of being a Christian, have a look at Hugh Miller: *The Footprints of the Creator: or, The Asterolepis of Stromness*[45] or *The Testimony of the Rocks: or, Geology in its Bearings on the Two Theologies, Natural and Revealed.*[46]

Some other populist science books that I have found helpful include Steve Jones, *In the Blood: God, Genesis and Destiny;*[47] Steven Hawking, *A Brief History of Time;*[48] Matt Ridley *Genome: The Autobiography of a Species in 23 Chapters;*[49] and especially Paul Davies *The Mind of God: Science and the Search for Ultimate Meaning,*[50] and *The Goldilocks Enigma: Why is the Universe Just Right for Life?*[51] Whilst Paul Davies is not a theist I have found him to be very fair and he does not dismiss theism – indeed he puts forward an excellent case for it. His books stretched my mind and in so doing reinforced my faith.

There are a number of scientists who are committed Christians and who have written about the interaction between their work and their faith. John Polkinghorne's *Quarks, Chaos and Christianity: Questions to Science and Religion*[52] is stimulating and thought-provoking as well. Owen Gingerich's *God's Universe*[53] is a small but well worthwhile book from a senior Astronomer. R. J. Berry's *God and the Biologist*[54] gives a theistic evolutionary viewpoint. My personal favourite (even though I do not agree with everything in it) is Francis Collins'

[45] University of Michigan University Library (1858)
[46] Available from http://www.openlibrary.org/details/testimonyoftherocks00mi llrich (1857)
[47] HarperCollins (1996)
[48] Bantam (1995)
[49] Fourth Estate (2000)
[50] Penguin (2006)
[51] Allen Lane (2006)
[52] Crossroad Publishing Co., USA (2005)
[53] The Belknap Press (2006)
[54] Apollos (1996)

The Language of God: a Scientist Presents Evidence for Belief.[55] It is one of the most interesting and faith-affirming books I have ever read.

Although many scientists would not agree with the Intelligent Design Movement (including many who accept that there is evidence for intelligent design) no-one should comment on it without reading Michael Behe's *Darwin's Black Box: Biochemical Challenges to Evolution.*[56] Likewise there are scientists and many Christians who adopt a young-earth creationist position. The best defence I have read of this is Douglas F. Kelly, *Creation and Change.*[57]

There are so many books that could be mentioned on Christianity, theology and morality. C. S. Lewis' *Mere Christianity*[58] and also his *Surprised by Joy*[59] remain wonderful explanations of many aspects of the Christian faith. Lee Strobel's *The Case for Christ: a Journalist's Personal Investigation of the Evidence for Jesus*[60] makes a good case. McGrath's *Christian Theology: An Introduction*[61] is the most reliable standard text book, whilst if you want a really reliable and in-depth systematic biblical theology it would be hard to beat Robert Duncan Culver's *Systematic Theology.*[62] John Stott's *Issues Facing Christians Today*[63] is a superb example of how to apply the Bible to modern life. On the other hand, *Godless Morality: Keeping Religion Out of Ethics*[64] by Richard Holloway is an example of how far the Church can wander away from the Christian faith, whilst Richard Bauckham's *God and the Crisis of Freedom: Biblical and*

[55] Simon & Schuster Ltd (2006)
[56] Simon & Schuster Ltd (1996)
[57] Mentor/Christian Focus Publications (1997)
[58] Fount (1997)
[59] Fount (1998)
[60] Zondervan (1998)
[61] Blackwell Publishers, 3rd edition (2001)
[62] Mentor/Christian Focus Publications (2005)
[63] Zondervan Publishing House, 4th edition (2006)
[64] Canongate Books Ltd (2000)

Contemporary Perspectives[65] contains an excellent chapter dealing with Holloway's book. John Wenham's *The Enigma of Evil: Can We Believe in the Goodness of God?*[66] is a tremendous discussion about some of the major issues as is Miroslav Volf's *Exclusion and Embrace: Theological Exploration of Identity, Otherness and Reconciliation.*[67] And I have always enjoyed reading F. F. Bruce – *The New Testament Documents: Are They Reliable?*[68] and his *The Hard Sayings of Jesus.*[69] Personally I have gained a lot from Augustine's *Confessions* and his *City of God.* Calvin's *Institutes* and anything by Jonathan Edwards will always repay the effort.

On the whole question of the 20th century being the failed century of atheism the best place to begin is Niall Ferguson, *The War of the World: History's Age of Hatred.*[70] Eric Hobsbawm's *Age of Extremes: The Short Twentieth Century 1914–1991*[71] is a standard work in the same vein. If you have any doubt about the atheism of Stalin or Mao then I would recommend Simon Sebag-Montefiore's *Stalin: The Court of the Red Tsar*[72] and Jung Chang's *Mao: The Unknown Story.*[73] On the rise of Nazism and Hitler's atheism have a look at Daniel Jonah Goldhagen, *Hitler's Willing Executioners,*[74] Gitta Sereny, *Albert Speer: His Battle with Truth,*[75] Ian Kershaw's *Hitler*[76] and Traudl Junge's *Until the Final Hour: Hitler's Last Secretary.*[77] To see how a Christian dealt with

[65] West-minster/John Knox Press, USA, 1st edition (2002)

[66] Inter-Varsity Press (1985)

[67] Abingdon Press, USA (1994)

[68] Inter-Varsity Press (2000)

[69] Hodder Christian Essentials, Hodder & Stoughton (1998)

[70] Allen Lane (2006)

[71] Abacus (1998)

[72] Phoenix Press (2004)

[73] Jonathan Cape (2005)

[74] Abacus (1997)

[75] Picador (1996)

[76] *Hitler 1889-1936, Hubris,* Penguin (1998); *Hitler 1936-1945, Nemesis* Penguin (2000)

[77] Weidenfeld & Nicolson (2003)

the evil of Nazism read Dietrich Bonhoeffer's *Discipleship*[78] and *Letters and Papers from Prison*.[79]

Two other works mentioned are Patrick Sookhdeo's article *The Myth of Moderate Islam*,[80] and Hans Rookmaaker's book *Modern Art and the Death of a Culture*.[81]

However, these letters have not just come out of science, theological, philosophical or history books. There are many other things that need to be added to the mix. I should also mention films that I have found to be stimulating and informative: *Schindlers List, Apocalypse Now, The Matrix* and *Downfall*. In terms of human nature and describing the problems that modern society faces *Crash* is thought-provoking and disturbing. *The World at War* is the best TV/DVD series made on the subject.

Music and poetry are two of the greatest gifts given to humans. Leonard Cohen, John Lennon, B. B. King, U2, Mozart, Emmylou Harris and Johnny Cash are the soundtrack of this book! Poems such as Leonard Cohen's *All There is to Know about Adolf Eichmann* say in a few words what I say in many!

In terms of novels I would recommend the following in particular: Dostoevsky's *The Brothers Karamazov*, the final part of C. S. Lewis' science fiction trilogy *That Hideous Strength* (which brilliantly warns us about the dangers of a godless scientific materialism), Nick Hornby's *About a Boy*, Albert Camus' *L'Etranger*, Douglas Coupland's *Girlfriend in a Coma* and Marilynn Robinson's beautifully written and wonderfully perceptive *Gilead*.

There are also numerous articles/reviews and booklets that I have read. One I would certainly want to recommend is a sermon published as a booklet by Alec MacDonald of

[78] Augsburg Fortress (2003)
[79] Pocket Books, enlarged 1st Touchstone edition (1997)
[80] The *Spectator*, 30 July 2005
[81] Apollos (1994)

Buccleuch and Greyfriars Free Church in Edinburgh – *Why I am not an Atheist*. Go to the Free Church website (www.freechurch. org) in order to get a copy.

Speaking of which, the Web is an excellent source of information, although please be careful about using *Wikipedia* and *Google* as shortcuts to actually finding out and thinking about things for yourself. (I have lost track of the number of times I have read 'scholars' who prove that this part of the Bible is false or that part is wrongly translated, usually by people who have never read a word of Greek or Hebrew in their life but suddenly 'know' because of something they have read on the web!) Some of the other websites I have used are the Faraday Institute – (www.st-edmunds.cam.ac.uk/faraday/index.php, an excellent source of material from Cambridge on the faith/science interaction), Christians in Science (www. cis.org.uk), Cees Dekker (www.mb.tn.tudelft.nl/user/dekker/index.html), Redeemer PCA (www.redeemer.com, a constant source of stimulation and encouragement as is John Piper, www.desiringgod.org). And of course I must not forget Richard Dawkins' own website (www.richarddawkins.net).

Prospect magazine, *Time,* The *Spectator,* The *Times,* The *Guardian* and The *New York Times* online often have excellent articles discussing many of the issues raised in these letters.

The originals of these letters and some of the responses to them can be found on the Free Church website (www. freechurch.org). The initial letter was posted on the Dawkins website and got such a vitriolic response that none of the others was posted there. I have however enjoyed corresponding with a number of atheist thinkers who in general have been a great deal more gracious and helpful. Most of our discussions tend to get bogged down in presuppositions. Atheists presuppose there is nothing outside matter. They tend to be logical positivists who demand proof but then set unreasonable limits as to what they will accept as proof. They reject totally the concept of revelation. Like atheists, I too presuppose that matter is real but I do not presuppose that matter is the *only* reality and I cannot *de facto* reject the concept of revelation out of hand. Indeed, that is one thing I have become more certain of – that despite the testimony of God in the creation ('For since the creation of the world God's invisible qualities – his eternal power and divine nature – have been clearly seen, being understood from what has been made', Romans 1:20) it is all the more necessary for the Spirit of God to work in our lives so that we may see. After all, did Jesus not say that unless a man was born of the Spirit he could not even see, never mind enter, the kingdom of God (John 3)?

In a sense I am grateful to Richard Dawkins for writing his book. It has made me think and has stretched my mind. Occasionally the book has angered me, and I am sorry if that sometimes has come across in these letters. (Perhaps I should point out that no atheists were harmed in the making of this book!) More often than not it has saddened me – I thought that Bertrand Russell was the most depressing atheist I had ever read but Dawkins beats him hands down – take for example this from *River Out of Eden: a Darwinian View of Life*:[82]

> We are survival machines – robot vehicles blindly programmed to preserve the selfish molecules known as genes. Our genes made us. We animals exist for their preservation and are nothing more than throwaway survival machines. The world of the selfish gene is one of savage competition, ruthless exploitation, and deceit.

What a desperate, sad and ugly world.

I am not surprised that Dawkins was 'mortified' by the fact that *The Selfish Gene*[83] is the favourite book of Jeff Skilling, the

[82] Phoenix Press (1996)
[83] Oxford University Press, 3rd revised edition (2006)

disgraced CEO of the Enron Corporation, and of course I realise that Dawkins is not a Social Darwinist. However I do not see how his social and political position is logically consistent with his philosophical position. My passion against what Dawkins is teaching is not driven out of some desire to protect or defend God. If God was a human construct then he would not be worth defending. If he is for real then he can defend himself. I am reminded of the famous Baptist minister C. H. Spurgeon who once retorted to a comment about him defending the Bible: 'Defend the Bible? I would as soon defend a lion!' No, my passion is simply that I have no doubt that if atheist philosophy gets an ever-increasing grip on Europe or the USA then we are really heading for another Dark Age.

For those American readers who think this may be true of Europe but can hardly apply to the USA let me remind you that the Church is only ever one generation away from extinction in any one area. I am not convinced that the USA Church is as strong as people suppose. Certainly, it looks as though the numbers are there but I suspect that much of it is very fragile and just as the European Church was largely unable to stand up to the assaults on the Bible that took place at the end of the 19th century, so the American Church, unless it wakes up and really does get back to the Bible, will soon find itself collapsing like a house of cards in-face of the onslaught of New Age spirituality, the cults, materialism and the newly confident militant atheism of Dawkins *et al.*

When I began this series of letters I had no idea where it was going to lead. I approached *The God Delusion* with a certain fear. Partly this was because whilst at University, I spent one year studying the English Civil War. I remember one black week when in reading the brilliant Marxist historian Christopher Hill I came across a statement to the effect that the English Puritans had engaged in the biggest brainwashing exercise in history. The thought crossed my mind: 'What if that is true? What if I too have been brainwashed? What if belief in God is just a delusion?' Twenty-five years later I sat down to read Dawkins' book. I tried to be as open-minded as possible. I approached it with twenty-five years more knowledge, knowledge of things that would strengthen my belief, and knowledge of things that would cause me to question my belief. Believe it or not the top three things that have caused me the most doubt have been some of the more difficult passages in the Bible, the Church and the God Channel. I have never really had any problem with the God vs. science dichotomy, which has always struck me as a false dichotomy – something that Dawkins illustrates almost more than anybody. And I still believe. Indeed I believe more than ever. If anything Dawkins' book has not only confirmed to me the barrenness of the wastelands of atheism but has caused me to be even more thankful to God for his glory, his truth, his universe, his Word and, most of all, his Son.

I have been challenged myself many times by atheists as I have been writing these letters: 'Prove it. Prove that God exists.' And I have told each of them that when I came to the end I would attempt to answer the question. I do so in the knowledge that it is impossible to prove God, not because he is unprovable, but because of our presuppositions. For example, if you believe that miracles don't happen then miracles will never be accepted by you as proof. When I went through that period of doubt 25 years ago it was the blackest period of my life, not because I could not see the attraction in not believing, but rather because I could. But what I knew then and what I know now will not allow me to turn away from God. It may be comforting to be an unbeliever (especially if you have been traumatised or let down by some religion or religious group) but what good does that do if your unbelief is not true? What if it is not the Christians who are deluded but the non-believers?

What then do I know? Why believe that Christianity is true? I can only list the following – all of which have been mentioned and discussed in the ten letters.

1. The Creation. By that I mean the heavens and the earth, from the smallest atom to the vastest galaxy. It all shouts to me of the glory of God. As I write I am sitting in my parents' home in the Scottish Highlands overlooking the Dornoch Firth. The night is still and clear and in a moment I will go and clear my head and gaze up at the stars.

   'The heavens declare the glory of God; the skies proclaim the work of his hands. Day after day they pour forth speech; night after night they display knowledge. There is no speech or language where their voice is not heard. Their voice goes out into all the earth, their words to the ends of the world. In the heavens he has pitched a tent for the sun' (Psalm 19:1-4).

   I include science in this category. I think it is very foolish for Christians or others to seek to prove or disprove God on the basis of a current scientific theory or on empirical evidence alone. But science within its own constraints as the observation of what God has made is a marvellous and often faith-affirming thing.

2. The Human mind and spirit. Why are we conscious? Why are we special? And life. Where does it come from? How can we get life from non-life?

3. The Moral Law. How do we know what good and evil are? Why do we have a sense of that at all?

4. Evil. Unlike Dawkins I cannot believe in the innate goodness of human beings. I see too much evil and no explanation fits what I observe as neatly and realistically as the teaching of the Bible. More than that I find that the Bible also brings us the answer to evil – and I have never yet come across any philosophy which does so.

5. Religion. Yes there is so much in religion that is wrong and in many ways I hate religion. Generally I think it is a human imitation that more often than not blocks the way to God rather than opens it. And yet it is an imitation of something that is real. As Augustine said, 'Our hearts were made for you, O God, and they are restless until they find their rest in you.'

6. Experience. I believe because I have tasted that God is good. Of course we can be deluded in our experience (that is why we need to reflect). And we can be wrong in our knowledge. But it would be a strange kind of person who did not take into account their experiences as part of the whole package. Not long after I became a Christian I was visiting a 'hippy' home where amidst all the music and drugs paraphernalia there was a poster stuck on the wall. Its words have remained with me ever since: 'All that I have seen teaches me to trust the Creator for all that I have not seen'. Sure – answered prayer, that sense of God's presence and that joy in worship may all have been illusory. But then again it may all have been real.

7. History. Again as I have continued to read and study history it has broadened my horizons and enables me to see in the words of the old cliché that it is 'His Story'. The history of mankind makes a whole lot more sense when it is set in the context of the history of God.

8. The Church. I mentioned earlier that there are things in the Church that more than anything else have caused me to doubt. When you see Christians behaving in a way which would shame Satanists, when you see preachers being pompous, hypocritical, money and glory-grabbers, then it is enough to put you off Christianity for life. But I have also seen the other side. I have seen the most beautiful people (some of whom had been quite frankly ugly before their conversion) behave in the most wonderful, inexplicable ways. Inexplicable that is except for the grace and love of God. The Church at its best is glorious, beautiful and one of the best reasons to believe.

9. The Bible. Again I mentioned problems that I have had and occasionally still have. But I can truthfully say this – that every year I read the Bible through at least once, that every day I try to read it and every week I study it in order to proclaim it. It has been a source of challenge, comfort, truth and renewal. I have no doubt that God speaks to me through it (and I don't mean the kind of loopy ignoring of context or more esoteric interpretations). In fact, I am so assured of this, experiencing it continually, that I have very little time for Christians who are always looking for 'extra words' – as though the Bible were not enough. For me the thrill is still there.

10. Jesus. I guess that any one of the above nine reasons would not be enough on their own – although I think their cumulative effect is overwhelming. But this is the icing on the cake. Actually no ... this *is* the cake. Jesus is the reason I believe and will continue to believe. 'In the past God spoke to our forefathers through the prophets at many times and in various ways, but in these last days he has spoken to us by

his Son, whom he appointed heir of all things, and through whom he made the universe. The Son is the radiance of God's glory and the exact representation of his being, sustaining all things by his powerful word' (Hebrews 1:1-3). All things were created by Christ, and for Christ. In him all things hold together (Colossians 1:17; Hebrews 1:3). It is in Christ that 'are hidden all the treasures of wisdom and knowledge' (Colossians 2:3). We hear about Jesus. We believe him. We receive him as Lord. We continue to live in him, 'rooted and built up in him, strengthened in the faith as you were taught, and overflowing with thankfulness' (Colossians 2:7). We are warned: 'See to it that no-one takes you captive through hollow and deceptive philosophy, which depends on human tradition and the basic principles of this world rather than on Christ' (Colossians 2:8). Would I really want to trade Jesus Christ for the Selfish Gene? No thanks. 'For in Christ all the fullness of the Deity lives in bodily form, and you have been given fullness in Christ.' Why would I swap the fullness of Jesus Christ for the emptiness of a universe and life without God?

And why should you? The wonderful thing about Jesus Christ is that you cannot inherit him, he cannot be bought and you cannot earn him. He simply comes as a free gift to all who would receive him. I leave you with some words from another man who had his life changed by Jesus and I pray that you too will see, believe and be changed.

In the beginning was the Word, and the Word was with God, and the Word was God. He was with God in the beginning. Through him all things were made; without him nothing was made that has been made. In him was life, and that life was the light of men. The light shines in the darkness, but the darkness has not understood it ... The true light that gives light to every man was coming into the world. He was in the world, and though the world was made through him, the world did not recognise him. He came to that which was his own, but his own did not receive him. Yet to all who received him, to those who believed in his name, he gave the right to become children of God – children born not of natural descent, nor of human decision or a husband's will, but born of God (John 1:1-5 and 9-13).

If you want to know more, just ask. Pray to God, seek his face and his forgiveness and he will never turn you away.

This book has been part of a conversation. One that is ongoing. It's not just about talk; it's about truth, life, meaning, beauty, justice and eternal love. And You. Join in.

Yours, etc.
David

David Robertson
St Peter's Free Church
4 St Peter's Street
Dundee
DD1 4JJ
Scotland, UK

Website – www.stpeters-dundee.org
(we have set up a section to discuss
the issues raised in these letters)

Email – david.robertson@freechurch.org

Christian Focus Publications

publishes books for all ages

Our mission statement –

STAYING FAITHFUL

In dependence upon God we seek to help make His infallible Word, the Bible, relevant. Our aim is to ensure that the Lord Jesus Christ is presented as the only hope to obtain forgiveness of sin, live a useful life and look forward to heaven with Him.

REACHING OUT

Christ's last command requires us to reach out to our world with His gospel. We seek to help fulfil that by publishing books that point people towards Jesus and help them develop a Christ-like maturity. We aim to equip all levels of readers for life, work, ministry and mission.

Books in our adult range are published in three imprints.

Christian Focus contains popular works including biographies, commentaries, basic doctrine and Christian living. Our children's books are also published in this imprint.

Mentor focuses on books written at a level suitable for Bible College and seminary students, pastors, and other serious readers. The imprint includes commentaries, doctrinal studies, examination of current issues and church history.

Christian Heritage contains classic writings from the past.

Christian Focus Publications, Ltd
Geanies House, Fearn,
Ross-shire, IV20 1TW, Scotland, United Kingdom
info@christianfocus.com